A
RICH
FEAST

By Chad Walsh

Behold the Glory
Campus Gods on Trial
C. S. Lewis: Apostle to the Skeptics
Doors into Poetry
Early Christians of the 21st Century
Eden Two-Way
The End of Nature
The Factual Dark
Faith and Behavior *(with Eric Montizambert)*
From Utopia to Nightmare
Garlands for Christmas
God at Large
Hang Me Up My Begging Bowl
The Honey and the Gall
Knock and Enter
The Literary Legacy of C. S. Lewis
Nellie and Her Flying Crocodile
The Psalm of Christ
A Rich Feast: Encountering the Bible
from Genesis to Revelation
The Rough Years
Stop Looking and Listen: An Invitation to the Christian Life
Today's Poets
Twice Ten *(with Eva Walsh)*
The Unknowing Dance
Why Go to Church? *(with Eva Walsh)*

A

RICH

FEAST

*Encountering the Bible
from Genesis to Revelation*

Chad Walsh

1817

Harper & Row, Publishers, San Francisco

*Cambridge, Hagerstown, Philadelphia, New York
London, Mexico City, São Paulo, Sydney*

for Esther M. Doyle

FIRST EDITION

Designed by Catherine Hopkins

Library of Congress Cataloging in Publication Data
Walsh, Chad.
   A rich feast.
   1. Bible—Criticism, interpretation, etc. I. Title.
BS511.2.W34   1981   220.6   80-8356
ISBN 0-06-069249-9

81 82 83 84 85 10 9 8 7 6 5 4 3 2 1

❋ CONTENTS ❋

PART THREE
THE FIVE-ACT DRAMA

Preface

I have written the book I wish had been available to me when I first began reading the Bible a half-lifetime ago. I was as ignorant of its contents as any Polynesian islander experiencing his first visit from missionaries. When I began to delve in the black-bound book I was never bored, but I was frequently confused. It seemed a rich feast of myths, tales, historical accounts, and—most of all—superb poetry. But how did it all fit together?

I turned to the commentaries, and found two kinds. Variety 1 was a series of moral meditations on scriptural passages. Variety 2 was an attempt to help readers use the fruits of biblical scholarship as they worked their way through a book as long as a six-inch bookshelf. I knew I would use these commentaries eventually, but not yet. At my beginning stage, I would have been overwhelmed by the minutiae of scholarship.

What I needed was a short book that would encourage me to relax and dip into the Bible as fancy led me. In time, I could be more systematic. But for the moment, I mainly wanted to feel my way around in this formidable book. Perhaps the guide that I wanted already existed; at least I did not find it, and was left to stumble along as best I could.

When I belatedly came to write this present book, I had in mind the impact that the Bible has had on so many people who approached it without any religious or other presuppositions. Take, for example, the novelist Virginia Woolf. In a letter to the composer, Ethel Smyth, Woolf exclaimed, "I have 3½ mins: before settling down to read the Bible. Why did you never tell me what a magnificent book it is!"* These words come from one

---

* Virginia Woolf, *The Letters of Virginia Woolf, Volume V:1932–1935,* ed. Nigel Nicolson and Jeanne Trautman (New York and London: Harcourt Brace Jovanovich, 1979), page 366.

who had little patience with ordinary religious activities. But no barriers existed between her and the Bible itself.

A Rich Feast is written for the person who has had little or no experience reading the Bible. I begin with the assumption that a false reverence may inhibit the reader. He should—at first—pick up the Bible as though it were any other book on the coffee table. Let the Bible speak in its many ways. The reader may at one point discover he is reading a poem; another time he will be following a historical account of actual events; at times he may think he is reading an anthropological monograph. The Bible is as varied as the dozens of persons who, over a period of more than a thousand years, put its words down on paper.

Much of the Bible can be read from a purely humanistic viewpoint. Or at least it can be read that way for awhile. Gradually, a mysterious Presence begins to impinge on the reader's consciousness. It is better to let that emerge in its own time rather than go seeking it from the start. In this way, the reader will first discover what the Bible has in common with the major literature of the world before endeavoring to know what is distinctive about it.

This book is divided into three parts. Part One is a sampling of selections from the Old and New Testaments, chosen in such a way as to illustrate the literary variety of the Bible. The emphasis in this part is humanistic—to become aware of the Bible as a magnificent human and literary achievement.

Part Two is a return visit to some of the portions of the Bible discussed earlier. The aim now is to come to terms with the mysterious Presence or "X-Dimension" that one begins to recognize everywhere in the Bible.

The main section of the book is Part Three. I have attempted to choose parts of the Bible that—when they are put together—will be faithful to the central emphases and insights of the Bible. One of the most distinctive things about the biblical stance is that it sees God as active in history and in the most ordinary events of daily life. To provide a framework for outlining the relation between humankind and God, I discuss all this as though the Bible were the script of a five-act play whose ultimate author is God and whose actors include the dramatis personae described in the Bible—as well as the person who puts himself in jeopardy by reading the Bible and discovering himself upon the cosmic stage, as one actor among many. Thus the dynamics of my approach is, first, the Bible as literature, as history, as social studies, and so forth. Second, awareness that there is more to it than that; that a fourth dimension becomes apparent to anyone who reads the Bible over a period of time. And third, an attempt to understand the interrelation between God and humanity, not only as a deeply private thing, but also as their meeting in the context of the cosmic drama symbolized by my metaphor of the five-act drama. But by the time that discovery has been made, the reader no longer needs this slender introduction to a very thick book.

Finally, some odds and ends. There is a series of books called the Apocrypha that bridges the period between the two Testaments. The Roman Catholic Church accepts them as a canonical part of the Bible; Protestant churches omit them. Some churches, such as the Anglican, recognize their religious significance but do not use them to establish doctrine. I have omitted these books, not because of their slightly shaky credentials, but because it was all I could do to discuss representative books of the Old and New Testaments. The reader who wishes to explore the Apocrypha will find that many Bibles now include these highly interesting and valuable books.

We are living in a period of great Bible translations, and it seemed a good idea to recognize this fact by quoting from a variety of versions. The King James Version (KJV) is the literary masterpiece of the translations, but of course it does not reflect the scholarship of recent centuries. The Revised Standard Version (RSV) is a good attempt to achieve greater clarity while maintaining as much as possible of the poetic flavor of the King James. The New English Bible (NEB) is the most conversational and idiomatic of the five translations. The Jerusalem Bible (JB) and the New International Version (NIV) are middle-of-the-road in their style, aiming mainly at accuracy and clarity, but achieving sometimes a quiet eloquence.

And finally, a personal note. Many people have helped me

write this book, by sharing with me their own insights and suggesting portions of the Bible that lend themselves to discussion. These good friends are too numerous to be listed by name, but my hearty gratitude goes forth to them. And it goes also to my daughter, Sarah Parente, who in addition to her other skills is an uncannily reliable and perceptive typist, ever ready to catch me up when my manuscript did not make good sense.

CHAD WALSH

Part One

⟫ A ⟪

RANDOM
SAMPLING

❧ 1 ❧

Practical Wisdom

For a start, take the Book of Proverbs. It has the advantage of being rarely read or preached about. One can come to it ignorant and fresh.

These practical moral maxims are traditionally attributed to the fountainhead of wisdom, Solomon, but many of them are much after this time. Nor were they a monopoly of the Hebrew people. Similar proverbs are found throughout the Middle East and many may have been borrowed from such countries as Mesopotamia and Egypt.

After a brief prologue, the Book of Proverbs pictures the family setting of moral instruction (1:8–9*):

> Attend, my son, to your father's instruction
> and do not reject the teaching of your mother;
> for they are a garland of grace on your head
> and a chain of honour round your neck.

Immediately there comes a warning (vv. 10–16) about armed robbery, a temptation that seems to have been as frequent in ancient days as now:

> My son, bad men may tempt you and say,
> "Come with us; let us lie in wait for someone's blood;
> let us waylay an innocent man who has done us no harm.

---

* Biblical quotations in this chapter (and in following chapters where indicated) are from the New English Bible, © The Delegates of the Oxford University Press and The Syndics of the Cambridge University Press, 1961, 1970. Reprinted by permission.

Like Sheol we will swallow them alive;
though blameless, they shall be like men who go down to the
   abyss.
We shall take rich treasure of every sort
and fill our homes with booty;
throw in your lot with us,
and we will have a common purse."
My son, do not go along with them,
keep clear of their ways;
they hasten hot-foot into crime,
impatient to shed blood.

Armed robbery is obviously not a modern innovation. Nor are fornication and adultery. Proverbs is full of warnings, as in 5:3–6:

For though the lips of an adulteress drip honey
and her tongue is smoother than oil,
yet in the end she is more bitter than wormwood,
and sharp as a two-edged sword.
Her feet go downwards on the path to death,
her course is set for Sheol.
She does not watch for the road that leads to life;
her course turns this way and that, and what does she care?

The father praises marriage as highly as he denounces unsanctioned unions. Using highly sexual metaphors, he lauds the ideal wife (5:15–19):

Drink water from your own cistern
and running water from your own spring;
do not let your well overflow into the road,
your runnels of water pour into the street;
let them be yours alone,
not shared with strangers.
Let your fountain, the wife of your youth,
be blessed, rejoice in her,
a lovely doe, a graceful hind, let her be your companion;
you will at all times be bathed in her love,
and her love will continually wrap you round.

Frequently the most down-to-earth aspects of social morality are commended, as in 11:1: "False scales are the Lord's abomination; correct weights are dear to his heart," or 14:31: "He who oppresses the poor insults his Maker; he who is generous to the needy honours him."

At all times the authors of Proverbs reveal shrewd powers of observation. Like realistic novelists, they depict society as it is. Take, for instance, these observations (19:6–8):

> Many curry favour with the great;
> a lavish giver has the world for his friend.
> A poor man's brothers all dislike him,
> how much more is he shunned by his friends!
> Practice in evil makes the perfect scoundrel;
> the man who talks too much meets his deserts.
> To learn sense is true self-love;
> cherish discernment and make sure of success.

These are hard-bitten maxims. The wisdom imparted by these proverbs is perfectly familiar; it is the shared platitudes that are the glue holding any society together. One can imagine Confucius reading this wisdom of the Hebrew people and dissenting from it in only minor nuances. Occasionally a modern reader does discover advice that seems to reflect an almost vanished era, as in 23:13–14: "Do not withhold discipline from a boy; take the stick to him, and save him from death. If you take the stick to him yourself, you will preserve him from the jaws of death."

The good wife is commended throughout, as in the long eulogy in 31:10–31, which brings the book to an end. The portrait it not that of women's liberation, but neither are we called upon to commend a soulless drudge. The wife is her husband's partner in the economic life of the family. She makes linen, buys land from her earnings, and plants a vineyard. She is clothed in "dignity and power." But she is more than economic woman; she shares the task of imparting wisdom to the family. Nor is she unappreciated: her children and her husband sing her praises. The picture of a happy household, busy at its work, is charmingly sketched.

A person reading Proverbs for the first time may perhaps feel that a specific set of values is being taught as if there could be no doubt about its universal validity. This is in fact the case.

This collides with the modern relativistic mind and the desire of each person to create his personal decalogue. Will the moral codes of the future have to be of the multiple-choice kind? What would the authors of Proverbs have said to that? I can imagine them granting that some values are optional (e.g., vegetarianism), but that the basic platitudes are still necessary in any world in which people live together. A society that condones falsehood, violence, robbery, casual sex, and cheating is a society swiftly on the way out. In fact, the great value of Proverbs is that it focuses squarely on the most basic principles of social existence. One can even argue that Proverbs is a kind of sociological treatise, exploring the foundations on which any society must rest.

It is best, however, not to consign this delightful but neglected book of the Bible wholly to the social sciences. The little vignettes, as of a young man encountering a painted woman, are sharply etched and stay in the mind.

Proverbs is far more than a handbook of moral living, a series of packaged answers. It is the self-portrait of an ancient society. That world was in many ways different from ours. But not totally different. And it is sketched in such living language that we seem to be listening to an ancient Hebrew sage. He shares his insights with us; he helps us to recognize parallels from our own experience.

⇒ 2 ⇐

The Hebrew Anthology

In my discussion of Proverbs, I omitted one important fact. It is written in verse. Indeed, perhaps a third of the Old Testament and considerable portions of the New Testament are verse. The newer translations of the Bible usually print such sections with line divisions so as to indicate this fact.

Why this pull toward verse? The easiest explanation is simply that verse is easier to remember. "An apple a day / Keeps the doctor away" will linger in the memory longer than "Apples are good for your health." In a society where reading was not a universal skill, the artifices of poetry were an aid to the faltering memory.

But surely there must be reasons other than this purely practical one. It is interesting that most civilizations, as they create a written literature, turn first to poetry and only later to prose. It seems almost universal human experience that if you want to say something with maximum strength and nuance, you will be drawn toward the resources of verse. Many paragraphs from the novels of Thomas Wolfe make effective free verse when divided into sense groups. Even Charles Dickens, a master of prose, glides into blank verse (unrhymed iambic pentameter) when he comes to moments of maximum intensity, such as the funeral of Little Nell in the *Old Curiosity Shop:* "Along the crowded path they bore her now."

One blessed peculiarity of ancient Hebrew poetry is that it is *not* based on rhyme (as we understand rhyme) or on a fixed meter. It indeed has a kind of rhyme, but it is the rhyme of ideas, not of sounds. This kind of rhyme can be translated into any language. The King James translators rarely worried about capturing the poetic quality of the Psalms. Theirs was the holy responsibility to be faithful to the literal meaning of each verse. But as they achieved that goal, they incidentally translated the Hebrew poetry into effective English poetry. One can take the sense groups of a psalm, as rendered in the King James Bible, and arrange them so that the poetic pattern is quite distinct.

The most common pattern of repetition is a couplet in which the second line somehow echoes the first. It may be simply another way of saying the same thing. Or it may modify what is said in the first line, even contradict it. The essential thing is for the two lines to have something in common. Take, for instance, these lines of Proverbs 1:8*:

---

*Biblical quotations in this chapter are from the King James Version, the most poetic of the English versions. To emphasize their poetic structures, I have taken the liberty of breaking the quotations into lines.

My son, hear the instruction of thy father,
and forsake not the law of thy mother . . .

This is a very simple example. The two lines actually say the same thing, except that the father is singled out in the first line and the mother in the second. "Hear" = "forsake not" and "instruction" = "law." We have indeed a kind of rhyme but it is of ideas, not sounds.

Sometimes much more elaborate patterns are used.* Take, for instance, these six lines from a poetic passage in Isaiah 6:10:

> Make the heart of this people fat
>   And make their ears heavy,
>   and shut their eyes;
>   lest they see with their eyes
>   and hear with their ears,
> and understand with their heart. . . .

The key words here—the meanings that rhyme by repetition— are heart, ears, and eyes. Line 1 rhymes with line 6, 2 with 5, 3 with 4. If the poet had wished to introduce further variations, he could have used some synonyms; for example, "heart" in line 6 could be replaced with "mind."

So much for the special nature of Hebrew poetry. It is time now to look at some samples of that poetry at is greatest: the psalms. These are traditionally attributed to King David, who was renowned as a musician and poet. Some of the psalms are indeed from his hand, but most were written much later, especially after the deportation to Babylon. Ideas of authorship were looser in biblical times than today. To speak of "The Psalms of David" meant "Psalms in the tradition of David."

I will start with Psalm 29, one of the shorter psalms:

Give unto the LORD, O ye mighty,
give unto the LORD glory and strength.

Give unto the LORD the glory due unto his name;
worship the LORD in the beauty of holiness.

---

*For a useful discussion, see Ruth apRoberts, "Old Testament Poetry: The Translatable Structure," *PMLA* (October 1977). The Isaiah example in this chapter is taken from this essay.

The voice of the LORD is upon the waters:
the God of glory thundereth:
the LORD is upon many waters.

The voice of the LORD is powerful;
the voice of the LORD is full of majesty.

The voice of the LORD breaketh the cedars;
yea, the LORD breaketh the cedars of Lebanon.

He maketh them also to skip like a calf;
Lebanon and Sirion like a young unicorn.

The voice of the LORD divideth the flames of fire.
The voice of the LORD shaketh the wilderness;
the LORD shaketh the wilderness of Kadesh.

The voice of the LORD maketh the hinds to calve,
and discovereth the forests:
and in his temple doth every one speak of his glory.

The Lord sitteth upon the flood;
yea, the LORD sitteth King for ever.

The LORD will give strength unto his people;
the LORD will bless his people with peace.

This psalm makes use of the principle of parallelism, mostly
in the form of couplets. But that is not the only kind of repetition that is used with poetic effect: for instance, the phrase
"The voice of the Lord." It is like a musical motif, repeated
throughout the poem and forming a drumbeat background
against which various ideas are projected: "The voice of the
LORD is upon the waters"; "The voice of the LORD breaketh the
cedars"; "The voice of the LORD maketh the hinds to calve";
and so forth.

It is mostly nature in its powerful, even violent phases that
the poem celebrates. The psalm is one vast analogy. The
strength of the Lord finds its "objective correlative" through
vivid pictures of nature in its tumultuous moments. Cedars
break and skip like a calf; the wilderness is shaken.

It is as though newly created man is taking time to look for
the first time at the natural world all around him, and marvels
at everything he sees, whether the normal process of birth or
the sound of great trees falling to the ground. No one who has

felt the power of this psalm will afterward be able to think of nature as always placid and domesticated. It has a life and will of its own. It is a symbol, but more than a symbol. The broken cedars symbolize God's might, but they are also a part of the familiar world and meant to be responded to in all their concreteness. The person who reads this poem will forever afterward have an enduring vision of the unquestionable reality of the physical world in which we—as well as cedars, hinds, and calves—make our homes.

Nature in another mood is found in Psalm 65. The might and tumult of natural forces are recognized, but the emphasis is on the life-giving strength of nature. Here is the second half of this psalm:

> Thou visitest the earth, and waterest it:
> thou greatly enrichest it with the river of God,
>   which is full of water:
>
> thou preparest them corn,
> when thou hast so provided for it.
>
> Thou waterest the ridges thereof abundantly:
> thou settlest the furrows thereof:
>
> thou makest it soft with showers:
> thou blessest the springing thereof.
>
> Thou crownest the year with thy goodness;
> and thy paths drop fatness.
>
> They drop upon the pastures of the wilderness:
> and the little hills rejoice on every side.
>
> The pastures are clothed with flocks;
> the valleys also are covered over with corn;
>
> they shout for joy,
> they also sing.

It is quickly evident that this psalm makes use of the same principle of parallelism as the preceding one: for example, the beautiful closing lines: "The pastures are clothed with flocks; / the valleys also are covered over with corn," and "They shout for joy, / they also sing."

We see nature providing water through rivers and showers and encouraging the young crops to sprout. The abundance of nature, friendly to humankind, is further exemplified by flocks that cover the hills and by grain fields in the valleys.

This psalm illustrates one strong characteristic of Hebrew poetry and of the Hebrew sensibility in general: It is life-affirming, not life-denying. It is, in one sense, very materialistic—that is, it looks upon this planet with its myriad forms of life, and calls it good. Flesh is good; it can be abused, but, properly understood, it lives in harmony with spirit. Sexual love is good; food is good; the beauty of the world is good. One can almost hear the poet smacking his lips when he composed such lines as "Thou crownest the year with thy goodness; / and thy paths drop fatness." And the people agree: they shout and sing to celebrate the earth's abundance.

Some psalms keep one mood from beginning to end. Others abruptly shift along the way. One such is Psalm 104. For the most part, it is one long hymn of praise to the goodness and rightness of things. The universe is reliable and friendly. Every creature has its niche in the great chain of being. There is food and drink for animals and humankind alike. It is even a world in which there is "wine that maketh glad the heart of man" and "oil to make his face to shine." Each creature has his home: the stork in the fir trees, wild goats in the high hills. Young lions "roar after their prey" as they are programmed to do by their genetic inheritance; "man goeth forth unto his work and to his labour until the evening."

So the psalm progresses until almost the end, when abruptly it turns into an imprecation:

Let the sinners be consumed out of the earth,
and let the wicked be no more.

This abrupt shift in tone is followed by the concluding prayer:

Bless thou the LORD, O my soul.
Praise ye the LORD.

Give thanks to God; he will exterminate the wicked—this is the final thought.

In this particular psalm, the imprecation seems an after-thought. Sometimes the curse is spelled out in much more de-tail, as in Psalm 137, which begins with a poignant picture of exile and ends by commending infanticide as suitable revenge.

First, we see the exiles in Babylon, and the natives saying "Sing us one of the songs of Zion." The memory of Jerusalem floods the speaker's mind. How can he pick up his harp and lightly sing a song of "mirth"? All that he and his people have suffered floods his consciousness. In a hymn of hatred he con-cludes his psalm:

> Remember, O LORD, the children of Edom in the day of Jerusalem;
> who said, Rase it, rase it, even to the foundation thereof.
>
> O daughter of Babylon, who art to be destroyed;
> happy shall he be, that rewardeth thee as thou hast served us.
>
> Happy shall he be,
> that taketh and dasheth thy little ones against the stones.

These two "cursing psalms" are not the only ones of that cat-egory, but they are enough to pose some questions. How are we to reconcile such beauty with such horror?

It helps to remember that the Hebrews had real reason for bitterness. They had been conquered in a brutal war and had doubtless seen their own children dashed against the stones. They were living as exiles in a foreign land. Victors can be magnanimous; it is more difficult for the defeated. One may understand, if not praise, the consuming hatred in the second half of this psalm.

There is another factor to be considered. One of the charac-teristics of the psalms is the intensity and range of the feelings they express. There are no drab grays and pale pinks and mauves. Black and white and flaming red and gleaming green are the colors on the canvas. There are no inhibitions about ex-pressing the deepest (and sometimes most questionable) feel-ings. To make the sudden transition from praising the perfec-tion of the visible world to pleading that certain unnamed persons be evicted from it is not too startling, if one takes into account the psychological and emotional candor of these an-

cient poets and the people whose innermost longing and hatred they expressed. They take human feeling as it is, and do
not try to prettify it. The Book of Psalms is a vast repository of
accurate insights into what it means to be a human being.
There are the heights and the depths, the glories and the horrors; hope and despair, joy and desolation. To read the psalms
is to explore one's own hidden life and feelings.

The psalms are part of the world's greatest inheritance of enduring poetry. In these poems, humanity is set in the midst of a
world that is unmistakably real and solid. It is described in
ways that speak not merely to the mind but to all the senses.
But it does more than depict the outer world; it explores the inner one. We are led psalm by psalm, line by line, to join hands
across the gulf of time with the authors of these poems. What
they were is what we are.

≫ **3** ≪

All Is Emptiness

The two books already sampled are very different in tone.
Proverbs is a compendium of practical advice about living in
society. Psalms represents the towering ups and giddy downs
of human feeling. We groan with despair, weep with sorrow,
shout with joy, curse with hatred, often in the course of one
short psalm. And all the while we look about us with new eyes,
to behold the world that poetry and science alike reveal to us.
It is a world of fertile soil, upspringing life, birds in their nests,
animals in their lairs. It is also a world we never made. It simply *is.*

Now one way of describing the Bible—inadequate, of
course—is to say that it is a small library helping us to discover
ourselves. Proverbs against false weights may flash into my

mind when I am making out my income tax return. I may suddenly remember the young man and the alluring adulteress when, in middle age, I learn that it is not only the young who encounter such temptations. Or the person reading the Psalms and experiencing their range of feeling can easily find his own memory rehearsing the same feelings that the psalm expresses.

In the Book of Ecclesiastes the reader discovers another aspect of himself. Here is a book whose central theme is "vanity" (emptiness). It does not offer the briskly practical advice of Proverbs nor the blazing affirmations of Psalms. All is subdued, gray, very weary, as though life itself is more a burden than a gift. Who has not known such days?

Ecclesiastes is one of the newest books of the Bible, dating perhaps from about the third century B.C. It was written at a time when the experience of the Hebrew people, with their successive defeats and deportations, began to cast doubt on the simple equation of virtue and success, wickedness and failure. It also seems to reflect a growing individualism. The focus of Ecclesiastes is not on the family, tribe, or nation, but the solitary individual, trying to make sense of the only life he ever expects to have.

The author of Ecclesiastes has observed humanity, and sees little reason for exultation and hope. He is not counting on any meaningful life beyond the grave. Nor does he see any evidence that in their brief lives men are rewarded or punished as their deeds deserve. A racketeer can die serenely in bed, surrounded by his adoring family and friends; an honest worker may perish of hunger or disease. In such a world, what advice can a wise man offer? Simply to live a moral life, even if there are no rewards and punishments, and enjoy what moderate and legitimate pleasures are available along the way. And go, at last, into Sheol, where all pleasures end. Evidently some early editor felt that all this was cold comfort. He inserted a kind of happy ending (12:9–14). This affirmative conclusion, repeating the old conviction that good and evil will always receive their appropriate rewards, flatly contradicts the rest of Ecclesiastes. Indeed the final words just before the appended ending remain, "Vanity of vanities, says the Preacher; all is vanity."

Hebrew thought is usually linear. It takes time seriously.
First there is creation, then the history of mankind as symbolized by Adam and Eve, then the special history of the Hebrew
people; finally a vision of a redeemed humanity. The movement of time thus has meaning. Real things happen in history
and they have consequences, and history is advancing toward
some kind of culmination. Ecclesiastes stands out because it
does not view time in this way. It sees history as a vast circle;
time is a cycle, slowly repeating itself. Socrates has drunk the
hemlock before and will drink it again, so to speak. Thus the
world does not basically change. The wise man recognizes this
and is grateful for whatever satisfactions come his way, but
does not expect them to come all the time. He accepts the patterns he sees all about him (3:1–8*):

> For everything there is a season, and a time for every matter under
> heaven:
> a time to be born, and a time to die;
> a time to plant, and a time to pluck up what is planted;
> a time to kill, and a time to heal;
> a time to break down, and a time to build up;
> a time to weep, and a time to laugh;
> a time to mourn, and a time to dance;
> a time to cast away stones, and a time to gather stones together;
> a time to embrace, and a time to refrain from embracing;
> a time to seek, and a time to lose;
> a time to keep, and a time to cast away;
> a time to rend, and a time to sew;
> a time to keep silence, and a time to speak;
> a time to love, and a time to hate;
> a time for war, and a time for peace.

The Preacher's agony is that all men seem to be treated the
same, no matter how they have lived. They have their brief
hour on the stage; they go down into the darkness, the good as
well as the evil (9:2–6):

---

* Biblical quotations in this chapter (and in following chapters where indicated) are from the Revised Standard Version of the Bible, copyrighted 1946, 1952,
© 1971, 1973.

... One fate comes to all, to the righteous and the wicked, to the good and the evil, to the clean and the unclean, to him who sacrifices and him who does not sacrifice. As is the good man, so is the sinner; and he who swears is as he who shuns an oath. This is an evil in all that is done under the sun, that one fate comes to all; also the hearts of men are full of evil, and madness is in their hearts while they live, and after that they go to the dead. But he who is joined with all the living has hope, for a living dog is better than a dead lion. For the living know that they will die, but the dead know nothing, and they have no more reward; but the memory of them is lost. Their love and their hate and their envy have already perished, and they have no more for ever any share in all that is done under the sun.

Among the Hebrews, belief in some significant afterlife, in which the accounts of good and evil are settled, came very late. There are only scattered traces in the Old Testament. Any concept of immortality was more likely to be collective: the nation or the family lives on, though its members disappear into the meaningless darkness of Sheol where no rumors of life under the sun ever reach them. It was thus that the Hebrews (including the Preacher) did not have the comforting possibility of saying that the injustices visible among men "under the sun" will be punished in some afterlife. If the Preacher was going to live a moral life, obeying the commandments of God, it could not be out of hope for reward or fear of punishment. He does good simply because it is good. There is an ethical nobility about his willingness to follow God though he has no assurance that all accounts are balanced in the long run.

In a magnificent prose poem, the Preacher brings the strands of his thought together (12:1-8):

Remember also your Creator in the days of your youth, before the evil days come, and the years draw nigh, when you will say, "I have no pleasure in them"; before the sun and the light, and the moon, and the stars are darkened and the clouds return after the rain; in the day when the keepers of the house tremble, and the strong men are bent, and the grinders cease because they are few, and those that look through the windows are dimmed, and the doors on the street are shut; when the sound of the grinding is low, and one rises up at the voice of a bird, and all the daughters of song are brought low; they are afraid also of what is high, and terrors are in the way; the almond tree blossoms, the grasshopper drags itself along and desire fails; because man goes to his eternal home, and the mourners go about the streets; before the silver cord is snapped, or the golden bowl is broken, or the pitcher is broken at the fountain, or the wheel broken at the cistern, and the dust returns to the earth as it was, and the spirit returns to God who gave it. Vanity of vanities, says the Preacher; all is vanity.

Such are the final words of the Preacher. There is the faint hope of some ultimate meaning to human existence, but a far stronger certainty that life is simply what it is, and that all go down into the pit of oblivion. What makes this dark vision tolerable? Perhaps simply the beauty of its poetic language. If we must all go down into darkness, we take with us the memory (as long as we have memories) of moon and stars growing dim, rainclouds, scenes of city life, unspoken terrors, the picture of the silver cord that is snapped, the golden bowl that is broken, the shattered pitcher. The beauty of these images comforts us as our dust prepares for its return journey to the earth whence it came, and we hear the echoing words, "Vanity of vanities, says the Preacher; all is vanity."

When Ecclesiastes first began to circulate with the other books of the Bible, it must have seemed something of a scandal. It is not mentioned in the New Testament, and for a long time its canonical status was in doubt. Perhaps the traditional attribution of the book to Solomon finally won it official status. Or it may be simply that Ecclesiastes was retained because no one could deny its understanding of the human condition. It is not the whole truth, but an important part of the truth. Who has not experienced the emptiness of all things and yearned for easy solutions and answers—but found none?

One need not assume that the authors of the Bible soberly set out to picture all human feelings, hopes, and fears. That was not their prime purpose. But as a by-product of the gradual creation of the Bible, we have the full spectrum of human feeling. When the scholars and editors and clerical authorities finally sat down to decide what belonged in the Bible and what did not, they perhaps recognized themselves in the words of the Preacher, and could not bear to exclude him from the company of those who, in the process of creating holy scripture, also painted the collective portrait of mankind.

⁂ 4 ⁂

The Loyal Widow

We come now to one of the world's greatest short stories, The Book of Ruth, and it should be read—at least the first time—as exactly that. It is a marvel of compression, swift movement, and characterization.

First we have the time in the distant past—"in the days of the Judges." The situation is swiftly sketched. Famine is ravaging the land; people are fleeing to nations that have adequate harvests. One of the refugees is Elimelech, a citizen of Bethlehem. With his wife, Naomi, and their two sons, Mahlon and Chilion, they make the great move into Moab, a country traditionally at enmity with the Hebrews. Ill fortune strikes again with the death of Elimelech. The sons, however, adapt themselves to a strange land and take Moabite wives, Orpah and Ruth. Then another blow falls: the two sons die.

Naomi hears that the famine in Judah has ended. She and her daughters-in-law set out on the road back. It is interesting that her decision seems a practical one, not motivated by uneasiness at living in an alien land. Naomi's strength of character and her sturdy commonsense are already clearly established. She would be at home anywhere.

At the frontier Naomi advises her daughters-in-law to return to their mothers' homes and seek husbands. The young women protest; they want to follow her back to Judah. Naomi urges them to think it through. After all, there will be no brothers of their husbands whom they could marry and carry on the family. (By Hebrew law, descent was not always reckoned in biological terms. A kinsman who married a widow would beget children who were reckoned as the children of the deceased husband.) Naomi presses her point (1:11–14*):

> "Have I any more sons in my womb to make husbands for you? Return my daughters, go, for I am too old now to marry again. Even if I said there is still hope for me, even if I were to have a husband this very night and bear sons, would you be prepared to wait until they were grown up? Would you refuse to marry for this? No, my daughters, I should then be deeply grieved for you, for the hand of Yahweh has been raised against me." And once more they started to weep aloud. Then Orpah kissed her mother-in-law and went back to her people. But Ruth clung to her.

Ruth takes her stand in words that still echo (1:16–17):

> "Wherever you go, I will go,
> wherever you live, I will live.
> Your people shall be my people,
> and your God, my God.
> Wherever you die, I will die
> and there I will be buried.

Naomi has met her match in strength, and ceases to importune her daughter-in-law. They finally reach Bethlehem at the beginning of the barley season.

In chapter 2 the same brisk narrative pace continues. The Bible is often rambling and repetitious, but in the Book of Ruth the movement is swift and sure. We begin to know Ruth better, as we see how she meets the situation in which she finds herself. By Hebrew law she, like anyone else in need, has the right to follow the reapers and glean the grain that has dropped to the ground. Ruth frankly admits a double motivation when she says to Naomi (2:2), " 'Let me go into the fields and glean among the ears of corn in the footsteps of some man who will look on me with favour.' " This *could* mean simply that she

---

* Biblical quotations in this chapter (and in following chapters where indicated) are from the Jerusalem Bible, copyright © 1966 by Darton, Longman & Todd, Ltd., and Doubleday & Company, Inc.

hoped some landowner would grant her the right to glean, but in the context of the story, there is a hint of marriage in the word "favour."

By chance—but is it chance?—Ruth chooses a field owned by a relative on her husband's side. This is Boaz, a prosperous farmer. He is not her closest relative, but close enough so that he might feel some obligation to look after her.

When Boaz returns he inquires about the young woman who is gleaning, and learns who she is. He seeks her out and tells her to concentrate on his farm; it will be safer that way. He authorizes her to glean and he provides food and drink for her. He secretly instructs his servants to let some grain fall, so her task will be easier.

One gets the impression that Boaz is doing more than his charitable duty. He has a swiftly growing interest in this remarkable Moabitess. Certainly he has deep respect and admiration. When Ruth overwhelms him with thanks, he in turn praises her for her devotion to her mother-in-law and her courage in coming to a strange land.

Ruth tells Naomi of her adventures, and the latter reveals that chance or providence has brought her to a relative who—while not her closest kin—has some obligation to see that the land owned by Elimelech is not alienated, and that his line does not terminate.

The possibility of marriage begins to dominate the plot in chapter 3. Naomi, as practical as her daughter-in-law, gives this advice (3:1–4):

> "My daughter, is it not my duty to see you happily settled? And is not Boaz, with whose servants you were, our kinsman? Now tonight he is winnowing the barley at the threshing-floor. Come, wash and anoint and dress yourself. Then go down to the threshing-floor. Do not make yourself known to him before he has finished eating and drinking. But when he settles down to sleep, take careful note of the place where he lies, then go and turn back the covering at his feet [probably a euphemism for the sex organs] and lie there yourself. He will tell you what to do."

During the night Boaz wakes up, sees a strange woman, and asks who she is. She identifies herself, and asks him to spread the skirt of his cloak over her. This is tantamount to a suggestion of marriage. Boaz praises her for not going after a young man and for seeking to provide a descendant for Elimelech. He is ready to marry her, but points out that she has a still closer relative who has the first option. So Ruth sleeps at his feet all night long. When Ruth reports to Naomi, the latter says contentedly (3:18), "Wait, my daughter, and see how things will go, for he will not rest until it is settled, and settled today."

Naomi's understanding of Boaz's character is accurate. He is not one to agonize over decisions. The next day he goes to the city gate, finds the man who is more closely related to Ruth, and in the presence of ten of the city's elders explains the situation to him, asking whether he wishes to buy the land that belonged to Elimelech. The man is ready enough, but balks when told he would be acquiring Ruth at the same time. He fears this would jeopardize his own inheritance. The reader breathes a sigh of relief. Boaz now stands next in line.

The story moves swiftly to its conclusion (4:13–16):

> So Boaz took Ruth and she became his wife. And when they came together, Yahweh made her conceive and she bore a son. And the women said to Naomi, "Blessed by Yahweh who has not left the dead man without next of kin this day to perpetuate his name in Israel. The child will be a comfort to you and the prop of your old age, for your daughter-in-law who loves you and is more to you than seven sons has given him birth." And Naomi took the child to her own bosom and she became his nurse.

What genre of literature is the Book of Ruth? From the viewpoint of an anthropologist it would be a source of rich data on an ancient people living in the Middle East. Obviously, the tale was not written with this purpose, but along the way one learns a great deal about local practices and customs: the care of the poor, the organization of agricultural operations, the rules and customs that governed descent and inheritance.

But more to the point, the Book of Ruth is a superbly written short story, as tightly constructed as anything written in modern times. It is a *story*. But is it a *love* story? The word love is used to describe Ruth's feeling for Naomi, but where does it occur in the annals of Ruth and Boaz?

What all the characters are trying to do is guarantee family continuity and protect their real estate. Yet how callow and false that way of putting it rings! What the story appears to be saying is first things first; love can follow. And it follows rapidly. Indeed, Boaz seems to take a highly personal interest in the young woman from their first meeting. His devoted attention to her needs might spring from sheer goodness of nature. But it might also reflect a more than legalistic awareness of family obligations. None of this is ever spelled out explicitly, but anyone reading the story without a scholarly commentary close at hand will sense a deeper level of the tale, two people turning to each other not simply because custom demands it, but because they are also drawn sexually. In particular, in the climactic scene where Ruth lies at Boaz' feet and awaits the moment when he will wake up, it is impossible not to speculate about the thoughts going through her mind. Will he take advantage of her helpless situation? Will he reject her? Or will he accept her tacit proposal of marriage?

The Bible is full of accounts of wickedness and depravity; many of its narratives have no happy ending. The Book of Ruth is notable for the taste of goodness. Naomi is the proverbial tower of strength, seeking the best possible life for her daughters-in-law. She has a clear head on her strong shoulders. Certainly, we see no weak and wavering female. Ruth is equally clearsighted and forthright. Boaz is a remarkable portrait: a rich man who is spontaneously generous to the unfortunate—and also responsive to the needs and charms of a young woman from a foreign country that the Hebrews have long detested.

Because the characters are what they are, the story has a happy ending. Each does the right thing. As a kind of bonus, love is awakened along the way. The nineteenth-century concept of romantic love—an imperious passion that seizes two souls and makes them oblivious to family and possessions—is absent here. The decisions that must be made are all practical ones. But from the midst of practicality there emerges a love story that resonates through the centuries.

⋙ 5 ⋘
The Tragedy of Saul

Whether a historic Naomi, Ruth, and Boaz ever lived does not matter. The reader accepts them as vividly sketched human beings and follows the drama of their adventures. But many of the tales in the Old Testament deal with people who certainly lived—Abraham, Joseph, and Moses, to name but three. The imagination of centuries may have magnified their lives, but the events were there in the first place. In short, much of the Bible is history.

No narrative in the Old Testament is more powerful and moving than the story of Saul, the first king of the Hebrews. Its historical background is the Hebrew conquest of Canaan, under the leadership of various "judges." After several centuries the task was done (more or less). Then came the infiltration of the mysterious Philistines, who posed a threat that the loose government of Judges could not handle. A king was needed, or so at least the people thought, as they looked at the tightly-knit and mighty kingdoms all around them.

Samuel, a combination prophet, priest, and judge, initially opposes the idea. He passionately believes that the real king of the Hebrews is Yahweh and that the people are turning away from him in their yearning to be like the nations all around them. He sternly describes what a king will be like. In words that probably reflect the eventual reign of Solomon, Samuel warns (1 Samuel 8:11–14*):

"These will be the ways of the king who will reign over you: he will take your sons and appoint them to his chariots and to be his horsemen, and to run before his chariots; and he will appoint for himself commanders of thousands and commanders of fifties, and some to plow his ground and to reap his harvest, and to make his implements of war and the equipment of his chariots. He will take

* Biblical quotations in this chapter are from the Revised Standard Version.

your daughters to be perfumers and cooks and bakers. He will take the best of your fields and vineyards and olive orchards and give them to his servants."

The people will not listen. Finally, Samuel receives a revelation telling him to go ahead and anoint a king. This he does with a heavy heart. He expects the worst. It is not slow in coming.

The story of King Saul has a cast of characters of almost Shakespearean variety and intensity. First of all there is Samuel, who is convinced that the divine voice speaks through him and who will never listen to excuses. He is a gray eminence, watching Saul and rebuking him whenever he falls short of the divine will as interpreted by Samuel.

Saul, a head higher than other men and filled with mad courage, is tormented by inner doubts and misgivings. He vacillates between weakness and excessive severity. At his best he is an effective military commander. But in modern terms, he seems a victim of paranoia, suspecting enemies and traitors all about him.

Among the other memorable characters are Ahinoam, Saul's brooding wife; his willful daughter, Michal; and his idealistic son, Jonathan. And of course the Edomite Iago, Doeg, who cheerfully cooperates in Saul's basest acts. And finally, David. He has the blessed gift of always landing on his feet. The people love him.

Saul is proclaimed king in a solemn public ceremony, and things begin well, with a resounding military victory. But the scene soon darkens. The tension between Saul and Samuel colors everything. Finally they come to a definite break. Samuel passes along to Saul a revelation that the Amalekites, who had attacked the Hebrews several centuries ago, must be exterminated. This includes even their livestock. Saul obeys most of the command, but spares their king, Agag. Also, the soldiers slaughter the scrubby livestock and keep the good. Samuel now suddenly appears and confronts Saul (15:13–14):

> And Samuel came to Saul, and Saul said to him, "Blessed be you to the LORD; I have performed the commandment of the LORD." And Samuel said, "What then is this bleating of the sheep in my ears, and the lowing of the oxen which I hear?"

Saul stumbles his way through an apologetic explanation, but Samuel will have none of this. God's commands are to be obeyed literally. The prophet implacably tells Saul (15:28): " 'The LORD has torn the kingdom of Israel from you this day, and has given it to a neighbor of yours, who is better than you.' " From now on, Saul's course is downhill.

Samuel loses no time in locating that neighbor. Divinely inspired, he seeks out the sons of Jesse; he finds the one he is looking for when he discovers the youngest son, David, out in the fields taking care of the sheep. Samuel anoints him as the king-to-be.

Saul begins to be tormented by an evil spirit, and his attendants think that music might soothe him. They send for David, who is already famous as a musician. For a time his music does calm the ailing king. They are like father and son, and David is given the honor of being the king's armor-bearer.

As often happens in the Bible, which reflects multiple sources of information, there are two accounts of David's arrival at court. One is that already summarized. The other has to do with the giant warrior, Goliath. Saul proclaims great rewards, including the hand of his daughter, Michal, to anyone who can slay him. Armed only with a sling, David lays Goliath low. The enemy soldiers fall back in panic, and the Hebrews win a major victory.

For awhile, all is idyllic. Jonathan and David become devoted friends, and David is appointed the commanding officer. But this does not last. Saul begins to suspect the motives of David. It does not help when women emerge from all the cities of Israel, singing a popular song (18:7): " 'Saul has slain his thousands, And David his ten thousands.' " The next day Saul goes into a frenzy while David is playing the soothing lyre, and throws a spear at him, which fortunately misses.

In his madness, Saul tries to persuade Jonathan to kill David, but the two young men are now close friends. Jonathan warns David, and is temporarily able to bring about a reconciliation between Saul and David. It is abruptly terminated by another spear-throwing episode, and David flees from the court. Jonathan is his covert ally, bringing him information about the king's state of mind.

The murderous intensity of the king's fear and hatred are revealed in what happens in a provincial shrine located at Nob. In their wanderings, David and his followers come to the shrine and explain they are on the king's business, and need something to eat. The gullible old priest provides them with loaves of consecrated bread. Meanwhile the vicious Edomite, Doeg, is quietly observing these events.

Doeg eagerly tells Saul what has happened, and retribution is not long in coming. When Saul and his soldiers burst into the shrine and accuse the priest of treason, he is completely bewildered. How can he be faulted for aiding the king's son-in-law and armor-bearer? The king is now in a murderous frenzy. He orders his guards to wipe out the shrine and its inhabitants. When they refuse to commit sacrilege, he gives the command to Doeg, who gladly obeys. Not even children, not even oxen and sheep are spared.

David, meanwhile, has fled to the court of Achish, king of Gath, where he pretends to be a madman, hoping in this way to be safe. King Achish, watching David's spittle running down his beard, asks his servants why they have admitted this lunatic; doesn't he have enough madmen of his own? David soon leaves and begins a guerrilla life, always on the move, accompanied by the tattered ranks of the discontented.

From now on, David's relation to Saul becomes more and more problematical. He yearns for reconciliation, but circumstances could push him into the camp of the Philistines. Saul is still in pursuit of him. Once, when David finds Saul in a cave, he passes by the chance to kill him. Instead he pleads (24:9–10):

"Why do you listen to the words of men who say, 'Behold, David seeks your hurt?' Lo, this day your eyes have seen how the Lord gave you today into my hand in the cave; and some bade me kill you, but I spared you. I said, 'I will not put forth my hand against my lord; for he is the Lord's anointed.' "

Saul is momentarily moved by gratitude. He acknowledges that David is destined to become king, and David promises to spare Saul's family. But this reconciliation, like all the others, proves to be a limited one. Saul returns home and David goes once more to his stronghold. Meanwhile, Samuel dies and is mourned by the nation.

Since Saul is still pursuing him, David flees again to the court of the Philistine king, this time not as a madman. He is welcomed by Achish, who assumes that David is despised by his own people and has no choice but to be loyal to the Philistines.

A great battle between the Hebrews and the Philistines is shaping up. Saul tries by dreams, prophets, and lots to learn what the outcome will be. No answer. In desperation—any news, good or bad, is preferable to uncertainty—he seeks out a medium living at Endor. At first she is suspicious, for mediums have been banished from the country by a royal decree. Finally she consents, and Saul asks her to bring up the spirit of Samuel. An old man, enveloped in a robe, rises from the earth. Samuel scolds Saul for disturbing his rest. Saul tells Samuel of his desperate situation, and asks for advice. What he gets is this (28:16–19):

> "Why then do you ask me, since the LORD has turned from you and become your enemy? The LORD has done to you as he spoke by me; for the LORD has torn the kingdom out of your hand, and given it to your neighbor, David. . . . Moreover the LORD will give Israel also with you into the hand of the Philistines; and tomorrow you and your sons shall be with me; the LORD will give the army of Israel also into the hand of the Philistines."

Saul falls flat on the ground in a faint. When he revives, the "Witch of Endor" prepares food for him and his two companions. They then depart to prepare for the inevitable battle next day. Perhaps we can imagine Saul relieved rather than otherwise. In a sense, he has passed through death and beyond. He no longer has uncertainties.

As the climax approaches, the Philistine army commanders grow uneasy about David and his Israelite band. How can they be sure he will not, in the heat of battle, shift to Saul's side and thus win his forgiveness and favor? Reluctantly, King Achish orders David and his men not to participate in the battle.

The final battle is described with great economy of language (31:1–6):

Now the Philistines fought against Israel; and the men of Israel fled before the Philistines, and fell slain on Mount Gilboa. And the Philistines overtook Saul and his sons; and the Philistines slew Jonathan and Abinadab and Malchishua, the sons of Saul. The battle pressed hard upon Saul, and the archers found him; and he was badly wounded by the archers. Then Saul said to his armor-bearer, "Draw your sword, and thrust me through with it, lest these uncircumcised come and thrust me through and make sport of me." But his armor-bearer would not; for he feared greatly. Therefore Saul took his own sword, and fell upon it. And when his armor-bearer saw that Saul was dead, he also fell upon his sword, and died with him. Thus Saul died, and his three sons, and his armor-bearer, and all his men, on the same day together.

David, far away, hears of the battle's outcome, and composes for Saul and Jonathan a noble elegy. Here is the concluding portion (2 Samuel 1:24–27):

"Ye daughters of Israel, weep over Saul,
  who clothed you daintily in scarlet,
  who put ornaments of gold upon your apparel.

"How are the mighty fallen
  in the midst of the battle!

"Jonathan lies slain upon thy high places.
  I am distressed for you, my brother Jonathan;
very pleasant have you been to me;
  your love to me was wonderful,
  passing the love of women.

"How are the mighty fallen,
  and the weapons of war perished!"

Thus ends the story of Saul, who loved greatly, hated greatly, feared greatly, and suffered greatly. His tormented spirit is now presumably in Sheol, where he and Samuel share the final resting place.

Although the above provides only the skeleton of the narrative, it is at least clear enough for the reader to see several ways of looking at it simultaneously. It is first of all history. The events may have become elaborated and interpreted with the centuries, but they actually happened. The Hebrews are feeling the influence of neighboring peoples; in particular, they are attracted to the practical advantages of a monarchy.

Second, one can read this story for the rich information about the customs and values of the times. We see the shape of ancient wars, often accompanied by total destruction of the enemy; the role of the prophet in relation to that of a king; the lingering superstitions as when Saul visits the Witch of Endor. This tale introduces us to an ancient way of life as truly as the Homeric epics help us get the feel of Greek life in the heroic age.

Third, it is supremely great literature. What a play Aeschylus or Sophocles—or Shakespeare—might have made of this story! Behold Saul and his combination of tremendous strengths—marred by a mysterious fatal flaw. What is that flaw? Too little trust in the divine, Samuel would have said. A modern psychologist might say it was lack of self-confidence, some faulty sense of identity. Certainly Saul has the magnitude of a tragic hero, and his downfall, from throne to a medium's hut, is enough to sate any vengeful god.

Saul's weaknesses are the more evident because of the contrast with David. The latter simply does what seems best on any occasion, and everything works out right. Even when he becomes a guerrilla chieftain, he is saved from suspicion of treason when the enemy king conveniently removes him from the battle front. From David's first moment on the stage, the action of the drama moves in one direction only: the fall of Saul, the rise of David. It is as though Saul were a King Claudius, and upon his death Fortinbras, who has been waiting offstage, will take over the tormented kingdom and set it right.

Or one can imagine this story falling into the hands of a Homer, and what he might have made of the epic conflict of Saul and David, set in the midst of the history of the Hebrew people. But we need not lament that Homer probably knew no Hebrew and never heard the story. The unknown authors who put the account together in the Bible had a power and skill equal to Homer's in writing history, and they created the most perfect Hebrew prose epic.

❧ 6 ❧

The Beauty of the Bride—
and the Bridegroom

Like Ecclesiastes, the Song of Songs (also called the Song of Solomon, because of Solomon's great reputation as a poet) is another book not immediately welcomed into the Bible. It has no explicit religious theme, and is full of a happy sensuality expressed in beautiful but unabashed language. Inhibited readers of the Bible still have difficulty responding to this book. Probably it would never have become an official part of the Bible if readers had not gradually come to see allegorical meanings in its love language.

For the time being we can forget about the allegories and read the Song of Songs on its most literal level. It may be more than a cycle of love poems, but it is not less. It is like a little play or oratorio, in which the Bridegroom, Bride, and their friends take turns celebrating the splendor of human love.

Quite possibly, these poems were originally used as part of wedding ceremonies. But first and foremost, beyond all speculation and conjecture, we have before us a series of songs in which a Bridegroom and Bride put into words the beauty of their love. Near the beginning we have the Bride and Bridegroom speaking to each other, with interspersed comments by their companions (1:8 to 2:13*):

Bridegroom
    If you yourself do not know,
    O fairest of women,
    go, follow the tracks of the sheep
    and mind your kids by the shepherds' huts.

    I would compare you, my dearest,

---

*Biblical quotations in this chapter are from the New English Bible.

to Pharaoh's chariot-horses.
Your cheeks are lovely between plaited tresses,
your neck with its jewelled chains.

Companions
We will make you braided plaits of gold
set with beads of silver.

Bride
While the king reclines on his couch,
my spikenard gives forth its scent.
My beloved is for me a bunch of myrrh
as he lies on my breast,
my beloved is for me a cluster of henna-blossom
from the vineyards of En-gedi.

Bridegroom
How beautiful you are, my dearest,
O how beautiful,
your eyes are like doves!

Bride
How beautiful you are, O my love,
and how pleasant!

Bridegroom
Our couch is shaded with branches;
the beams of our house are of cedar,
our ceilings are all of fir.

Bride
I am an asphodel in Sharon,
a lily growing in the valley.

Bridegroom
No, a lily among thorns
is my dearest among girls.

Bride
Like an apricot-tree among the trees of the wood,
so is my beloved among boys.
To sit in its shadow was my delight,
and its fruit was sweet to my taste.
He took me into the wine-garden
and gave me loving glances.
He refreshed me with raisins, he revived me with apricots;

for I was faint with love.
His left arm was under my head, his right arm was round me.

Bridegroom

I charge you, daughters of Jerusalem,
by the spirits and the goddesses of the field:
Do not rouse her, do not disturb my love
until she is ready.

Bride

Hark! My beloved! Here he comes,
bounding over the mountains, leaping over the hills.
My beloved is like a gazelle
or a young wild goat:
there he stands outside our wall,
peeping in at the windows, glancing through the lattice.

My beloved answered, he said to me:
Rise up, my darling;
my fairest, come away.
For now the winter is past,
the rains are over and gone;
the flowers appear in the country-side;
the time is coming when the birds will sing,
and the turtle-dove's cooing will be heard in our land;
when the green figs will ripen on the fig-trees
and the vines give forth their fragrance.
Rise up, my darling;
my fairest, come away.

The Bridegroom praises his beloved's cheeks, "lovely between plaited tresses," and her neck "with its jewelled chains." The Bride responds, "My beloved is for me a bunch of myrrh as he lies on my breast." Or a little farther on, "His left arm was under my head, his right arm was round me."

We see the Bridegroom as he approaches, "bounding over the mountains, leaping over the hills" like a gazelle or a young wild goat. He exclaims, in language praising the fertility of nature, "The flowers appear in the country-side; the time is coming when the birds will sing, and the turtle-dove's cooing will be heard in our land."

Now soon follows a long song of praise, almost a physical inventory of the bride, as he exults in every aspect of her beauty (4:1–11):

Bridegroom
How beautiful you are, my dearest, how beautiful!
Your eyes behind your veil are like doves,
your hair like a flock of goats streaming down Mount Gilead.
Your teeth are like a flock of ewes just shorn
which have come up fresh from the dipping;
each ewe has twins and none has cast a lamb.
Your lips are like a scarlet thread,
and your words are delightful;
your parted lips behind your veil
are like a pomegranate cut open.
Your neck is like David's tower,
which is built with winding courses;
a thousand bucklers hang upon it,
and all are warriors' shields.
Your two breasts are like two fawns,
twin fawns of a gazelle.
While the day is cool and the shadows are dispersing,
I will go to the mountains of myrrh
and to the hills of frankincense.
You are beautiful, my dearest,
beautiful without a flaw.

Come from Lebanon, my bride;
come with me from Lebanon.
Hurry down from the top of Amana,
from Senir's top and Hermon's,
from the lion's lairs, and the hills the leopards haunt.

You have stolen my heart, my sister,
you have stolen it, my bride,
with one of your eyes, with one jewel of your necklace.
How beautiful are your breasts, my sister, my bride!
Your love is more fragrant than wine,
and your perfumes sweeter than any spices.
Your lips drop sweetness like the honeycomb, my bride,
syrup and milk are under your tongue,
and your dress has the scent of Lebanon.

One could go on to comment on individual lines of the "Greatest of All Songs" (which is what "Song of Songs" means), but that is not needed. Anyone simply reading the entire book without presuppositions will find in it unforgettable poetry. The love of man and woman is celebrated as one of the great goods of human experience. There is no smirking here, but also no false spirituality. No attempt is made to tone down the sheer physicality of that mysterious magnetism that draws two bodies together in union. The love of man and woman is seen as one with the beauty, abundance, and vitality of nature itself. There is no mention of sexual adjustment clinics or divorce courts. To be in love, to do the acts of love, is as right and natural as to feast at a banquet or taste of heavenly wines.

As one reads and rereads the Song of Songs, it begins to seem less an odd intruder in the canon of Scripture. The Old Testament in particular is a very earthy work. A Buddhist might well say this is the most materialistic of all great scriptures. He would not be wrong. The Bible presents and praises a physical universe inhabited by physical beings like squirrels and ourselves. The spectacle is good. Certainly, the physical universe can be abused. Strip-mining can destroy mountains; adultery can demean sexual love; joy at the rich feasts offered to our taste buds can slide into gluttony. But only our ingenuity permits us to pervert such inherently good things as food and sex. Wholly lacking is the shamefaced attitude that one often finds among the pious, as exemplified by the legendary mother who told her daughters that when they were married, it was their duty to accede to the gross appetites of their husbands, but "Don't you ever let me catch you enjoying it!"

The ethical system taught by the Bible is deeply influenced by the world-affirming stance of the ancient Hebrew people. To them such questions as whether interest could be charged on loans or whether the poor had gleaning rights were as basic to the moral life as the prohibitions against bearing false witness or walking off with a man's wife. The Old Testament, as we saw earlier, is a book that commands honest weights and measures as one practical way of implementing both "Thou shalt not steal" and "Thou shalt love thy neighbor as thyself."

But this discussion is becoming heavy. We started out with a glimpse at some of the most powerful and tender love poems ever composed, and before we knew what was happening, we were examining the basic mind-set of the ancient Hebrews. Firmly entrenched in the Bible we have a marriage hymn which does not call for the sublimation of our sexual instincts. It glorifies them and beautifies them with richness of language and a full-throated appeal to analogies from nature. Marriage is not, the Song says, an apologetic necessity to keep the race going, but a glorious fulfillment of these possibilities that humanity shares with the humblest creatures of the fields and forests. A shout of praise that we are what we are goes up to heaven, and we rejoice that our basic instincts can lead us to the most beautiful of human experiences.

ᐳ 7 ᐸ
Metaphorical Language and Deeds

Almost all the devices that poets use to present an idea or feeling powerfully can be found somewhere in Scripture. This does not mean that the authors of the Bible were aiming at a purely literary impact. They simply used the tools of poetry to convey an urgent message to their people with maximum strength. They often created memorable poetry without having set out "to write a poem."

One poetic device frequently found in the Bible is the "extended metaphor." It is based on an elaborate comparison that runs through a whole poem and gives it unity. For example, Shakespeare's sonnet 143:

Lo, as a careful housewife runs to catch
One of her feathered creatures broke away,
Sets down her babe, and makes all swift dispatch
In pursuit of the thing she would have stay;
Whilst her neglected child holds her in chase,

Cries to catch her whose busy care is bent
To follow that which flies before her face,
Not prizing her poor infant's discontent—

So runn'st thou after that which flies from thee,
Whilst I, thy babe, chase thee afar behind;
But if thou catch thy hope, turn back to me
And play the mother's part, kiss me, be kind.
So will I pray that thou mayst have thy Will,
If thou turn back and my loud crying still.

The poem sketches a familiar barnyard scene—the escape of a chicken and the mother's temporary neglect of her baby while she pursues the frantic fowl. The babe obviously stands for Shakespeare, the mother is his beloved, and the chicken represents a rival for her affections. The "babe" is pleading for some comfort once the "mother" has recaptured the "chicken" of her heart's desire.

To turn from this playful little poem to the words of Hosea is to move into a world of far greater intensity. But the same literary device is used to jab the reader awake and make him face his own attitudes.

The Book of Hosea comes from one of the early prophets. These were forth-tellers rather than fore-tellers; in other words, spokesmen for whatever final reality molds history. By being peculiarly attuned to that reality, they knew the laws that govern the great movements of history. As they saw it, a kind of divine justice prevails; that is, certain actions, decisions, ways of life inevitably lead to certain consequences. If you add two and two, you have to get four. If a nation becomes corrupt, blind to social needs, idolatrous, the laws of karma will bring it down unless it changes its ways in time. The function of the prophets is to analyze what is wrong, and to offer the chance of a change in the national course before it is too late. Often it seems that their message is mostly one of doom, but always they hold out the hope of a cleansed and renewed world if the nation will heed their advice. Though prophets are particularly associated with ancient Hebrew history, it is not farfetched to recognize prophets proclaiming similar appeals in our own times, such as the few people who, twenty years ago, predicted the exhaustion of energy resources if the nation did not repent and conserve.

But back to the extended metaphor. Hosea wanted some striking way to highlight the corruption of Israel, the threat of punishment, the possibility of reform. He could have composed a treatise like the essays on the Op-Ed page of the *New York Times*—and few would have paid any attention. He needed some way of reaching people on a gut level. What better way than to speak *as though* God were a husband married to a faithless wife? The themes of corruption, punishment, and rehabilitation can all be symbolized by this extended metaphor. But Hosea goes a step further. As do many of the other prophets, he performs a symbolic act. Biblical scholars have solemnly debated whether Hosea's wife became unfaithful after their marriage, or was a prostitute from the beginning. The latter is quite possible. Hosea, aflame with a message, may have deliberately wedded a harlot in order to act out an extended metaphor, dramatizing the relation of the Hebrew people to Yahweh. In any case, the first three chapters of the Book of Hosea are built around these analogies:

Yahweh = husband
Israel = erring wife
Israel's neglect of Yahweh = wife's adultery

The whole theme of Hosea's message is expressed in 1:2,* " 'Go, take to yourself an adulterous wife and children of unfaithfulness, because the land is guilty of the vilest adultery in departing from the LORD!' "

The narrative then goes on to list the three children of this unpromising union: Jezreel (the site of a political massacre), "Not loved," and "Not my people." In chapter 2, Yahweh continues speaking as though he were a wronged husband. He threatens punishment to his unfaithful "wife" (the Hebrew

---

*Biblical quotations in this chapter (and in following chapters where indicated) are from the Holy Bible: New International Version, © 1978 by the New York International Bible Society. Used by permission of Zondervan Bible Publishers.

people), but at the same time yearns for her reform and holds
forth hope of a renewed relation.

First, the threat of punishment (2:4):

> "Rebuke your mother, rebuke her,
>   for she is not my wife,
>   and I am not her husband.
> Let her remove the adulterous look from her face
>   and the unfaithfulness from between her breasts.
> Otherwise I will strip her naked
>   and make her as bare as on the day she was born;
> I will make her like a desert,
>   turn her into a parched land,
>   and slay her with thirst.
> I will not show my love to her children,
>   because they are the children of adultery."

Almost imperceptibly, the picture of the faithless wife
changes into that of a nation which has turned aside from its
true lord. Yahweh threatens to send famine and wild beasts, so
that at last the "wife" will admit she was better off with her
husband and should return to him. The vision then shifts to a
renewed world after the wife is back with her faithful husband
(2:14–15):

> "Therefore I am now going to allure her;
> I will lead her into the desert
>   and speak tenderly to her.
> There I will give her back her vineyards,
>   and will make the Valley of Achor a door of hope.
> There she will sing as in the days of her youth,
>   as in the day she came up out of Egypt."

He goes on to picture the new age that will be brought into existence by the reconciliation of "wife" and "husband" (2:18–
19):

> "Bow and sword and battle
>   I will abolish from the land,
>   so that all may lie down in safety.
> I will betroth you to me forever;
>   I will betroth you in righteousness and justice,
>   in love and compassion."

And he goes on to a climactic promise (2:23):

> "I will show my love to the one I called 'Not my loved one.' I will say to those called 'Not my people,' 'You are my people'; and they will say, 'You are my God.' "

Hosea carries on the extended metaphor through chapter 3, and then drops it. It has served its purpose, by vividly stating the infidelity of the Hebrew people toward their heavenly master. Hosea is then ready to spell out in more detail the specific sins of the Hebrews: cursing, lying, murder, stealing, adultery, idolatry—the list goes on endlessly. In direct language he warns of the punishment to come, and summons them to repent and reform. Shamefully as they have behaved toward their "husband," he is still willing to forget and renew.

When the Song of Songs was discussed, we noted the affirmative attitude the Hebrews had about the human body, sex, and marital love. The Book of Hosea reveals that this recognition of the glory of the flesh was not a late development. Long centuries lie between Hosea and the composition of the Song of Songs. When seeking a figure of speech to dramatize the relation between heaven and earth, Hosea was able to turn to the rich carnality of human existence and find in it a worthy parallel to God's fellowship with his creation. The more one thinks about it, the more daring the comparison seems. But here it is in Hosea, and through his book it has profoundly influenced later books of the Bible, and the very way one conceives of the ultimate mind and the heart of the universe.

❋ 8 ❋
"As If" Stories

To early humanity the world must have seemed a place of impenetrable mysteries. All about were the teeming forms of life, the successive stages of the seasons, a crazy quilt of nations and languages. It was not anything that our species set about to create; it was simply *there*.

Of course, we are not much better off. We can break the genetic code and measure the distance of the galaxies, but the ultimate questions elude us; especially the *why*. As much as the primitive, we are driven to say, "It might be like this." An example is the "big bang" theory of the expanding universe. Whether such an explosion ever took place remains a question that may or may not be answered, but at least the theory provides words by which we can talk about the mystery of there being any universe at all.

We are driven to create stories of the "as if" kind so we can discuss realities that would otherwise condemn us to silence. Because of Freud, we can talk about the ego and the id—yet we have never seen either. Or to take another example, we may know intuitively that humanity is in essence one race, though this unity is not revealed in the daily lives of the earth's inhabitants. We do not in fact behave like one big family. We speak mutually incomprehensible languages, and war upon one another like separate species. If we assume that original harmony and unity were the starting point, what went wrong? We cannot travel backward in a time machine to find out.

Stories that try to answer such questions are called myths. The word need not put us off. As used here and in all discussions in this book, it does *not* mean an idle tale. Rather, it signifies a story which sets out in an "as if" way to explain things that everyone is aware of, like mankind's brawling disunity. A myth is a kind of model, taking into account any empirical facts than human observers have noted, and trying to arrive by means of a story at a possible understanding of a phenomenon.

Genesis is the richest source of biblical myths, and one of the most haunting is the tale of the Tower of Babel (Genesis 11:1–9.*):

> And the whole earth was of one language, and of one speech. And it came to pass, as they journeyed from the east, that they found a plain in the land of Shinar; and they dwelt there. And they said one to another, Go to, let us make brick and burn them thoroughly. And they had brick for stone, and slime had they for mortar. And they said, Go to, let us build us a city and a tower, whose top may reach unto heaven; and let us make us a name, lest we be scattered abroad upon the face of the whole earth. And the LORD came down to see the city and the tower, which the children of men builded. And the LORD said, Behold, the people is one, and they have all one language; and this they begin to do: and now nothing will be restrained from them, which they have imagined to do. Go to, let us go down, and there confound their language, that they may not understand one another's speech. So the LORD scattered them abroad from thence upon the face of all the earth: and they left off to build the city. Therefore is the name of it called Babel; because the LORD did there confound the language of all the earth: and from thence did the LORD scatter them abroad upon the face of all the earth.

Is there a germ of historical truth in the tale? Clearly so, as is often the case with myths. The Assyrians and Babylonians were much given to building huge towers or ziggurats to proclaim their might. These have gradually decayed into the vast mounds that archeologists probe.

The unknown Hebrew author who wrote the story of the Tower of Babel was thinking of more than an architectural feat or simple display of imperial power and pomp. He saw the human, inner meaning of these frantic activities. And he saw the folly. Here were people who already possessed the most precious bond of unity, a common language. But that was not enough. They had to have more security and yet more, so that their most distant descendants could enjoy eternal safety and glory.

A Hebrew might gaze at the towers and see not just the obvi-

---

* Biblical quotations in this chapter are from the King James Version.

ous display of might, but also the inner unease that drives human beings to proclaim themselves to all eternity. They hoped to cheat time and fate, to prove the exception to the rule of history that nations come and go. The more surely men built barricades against the onslaughts of time, the more surely they moved toward their doom.

But at this point, the author of this myth must have asked himself: Am I so different? To one degree or another humankind clutches at its security, and in the process neglects such simple duties as compassion and justice. We can imagine this nameless author wandering among the missile silos of our western landscape and seeing in their provisions for "security"—and infinite destruction—an overweening pride and determination to control the movements of history. The tower-building passions of the historical Babylonians and Assyrians become symbols of the way all nations and individuals seek security, though it will prove illusory in the long run. The loss of a sense of unity and dedication to common causes that sensitive observers have noted in America these last few years suggests that no nation is immune to the inner decay that comes when security—for a nation, a class, a person—becomes so dominant a goal that all else is neglected.

Thus out of the provincial experience of observing their mighty neighbors laying their bricks in order to tower into the heavens, the author saw a broader meaning. The tower builders were and are us. They refused to make their spiritual home in the world that lay all about them—a world in which unity of speech made possible human understanding. They abandoned this unity when they reached too far for security, and were suddenly confronted with the forces of history driving them out into the corners of the earth, babbling in mutually unintelligible languages.

Well, if that is what the story is about, why did not the author tell it straight, as I seem to have done? Could he not have composed a short essay on the way the events of history limit our proud pretentions? The answer is, first, that the ancient Hebrews did not think in terms of formal monographs. They might write about sociological and psychological matters, but their language did not have these two words. They thought in terms of pictures and stories which—passing through the reader's imagination—gave him the symbols with which he could express himself. When he talked about a tower toppling, he might be thinking of "excessive emphasis on security," but if he had translated his symbols into such colorless language, the power and precision of his thought would have been weakened and deprived of its capacity to haunt the reader.

There is a further advantage of the myth as a way of saying things that cannot be as strongly stated in any other way. A myth is open-ended. It does not set up a neat series of parallels between the events in a story and our knowledge of the ordinary world and its events. I have told you what I see in the Tower of Babel story and why I find it still relevant. But someone else may read the same story and find it vibrating with different implications. Thus a myth of the biblical sort sets in motion the movements of the imagination—and of the intellect—and like an atomic reactor that is fueled to last forever, it generates energy and new insights as successive generations respond to it.

≫ 9 ≪

Daily Life and the Parable

In an earlier chapter we looked at the Book of Proverbs and found that it conveys traditional wisdom in the plainest and most direct way possible. There is no ambiguity about such a statement as Proverbs 11:1:*

False scales are the Lord's abomination;
    correct weights are dear to his heart.

---

*Biblical quotations in this chapter are from the New English Bible.

Nor does one have any difficulty in understanding 15:1:

A soft answer turns away anger,
  but a sharp word makes tempers hot.

There is a problem with such direct teaching. It is often a case of in one ear and out the other. The great moral teachers have always struggled to find ways of imparting wisdom in a less cut-and-dried manner. One extreme form of instructional indirectness is the Zen Buddhist kōan. A pupil is told, for instance, to meditate on the phrase, "The sound of one hand clapping." Months, even years later, the "answer" comes to him but it cannot be put into words. It is more an illumination, a state of soul.

A parable is the exact opposite of a kōan. A reader, once sensing the basic analogy, is able to summarize the purport of the parable in plain language. One asks, therefore, why not come right out and say things directly from the very beginning? Why put the reader through a kind of game? The answer may be that the rigors of the "game" compel the pupil to work his way to an interpretation—and as a result, he will remember it.

Parables are rarities in the Old Testament. The two stories that everyone agrees to call by that name are the parable of the unproductive vineyard (Isaiah 5:1–6) and Nathan's rebuke to David. This latter parable incidentally illustrates the unflinching candor of the Bible. David was the model for the hoped-for messiah, but the Bible does not omit the warts on his face.

The background of Nathan's parable is the wandering eye of King David. One day the monarch is strolling on the flat roof of his palace when he sees a beautiful woman (Bathsheba, wife of Uriah the Hittite) taking a bath. Events move fast. He sleeps with her, and soon learns she is pregnant. David solves this problem with kingly dispatch by writing a letter to his general, commanding him to station Uriah where the fighting is thickest and then suddenly fall back, leaving him to meet his death. After Bathsheba has dutifully finished her period of mourning, she moves into his palace and they are married.

The prophet Nathan, who seems to have been a kind of royal chaplain, hears of David's behavior. At this point, he could have confronted the King directly, saying, "You killed Uriah and now you have the effrontery to marry his widow." It requires little practical psychology to foresee the result—the king taken off guard, confused, defensive, probably dangerous. Nathan had to lead the king along one step at a time until he faced the enormity of his deeds. To accomplish this, Nathan tells a simple parable (2 Samuel 12:1–10):

> The LORD sent Nathan the prophet to David, and when he entered his presence, he said to him, "There were once two men in the same city, one rich and the other poor. The rich man had large flocks and herds, but the poor man had nothing of his own except one little ewe lamb. He reared it himself, and it grew up in his home with his own sons. It ate from his dish, drank from his cup and nestled in his arms; it was like a daughter to him. One day a traveller came to the rich man's house, and he, too mean to take something from his own flocks and herds to serve to his guest, took the poor man's lamb and served up that." David was very angry, and burst out, "As the LORD lives, the man who did this deserves to die! He shall pay for the lamb four times over, because he has done this and shown no pity." Then Nathan said to David, "You are the man. This is the word of the LORD the God of Israel to you: 'I anointed you king over Israel, I rescued you from the power of Saul, I gave you your master's daughter and his wives to be your own, I gave you the daughters of Israel and Judah; and, had this not been enough, I would have added other favours as great. Why then have you flouted the word of the LORD by doing what is wrong in my eyes? You have struck down Uriah the Hittite with the sword; the man himself you murdered by the sword of the Ammonites, and you have stolen his wife. Now, therefore, since you have despised me and taken the wife of Uriah the Hittite to be your own wife, your family shall never again have rest from the sword.' "

All David's defenses are now in ruins. "I have sinned against the LORD," he confesses without further excuses or evasions.

By the time of Jesus, the parable was a common teaching device of the rabbis. Jesus used it as his favorite, but not exclusive, means of instruction. Sometimes he is very direct, as in the Beatitudes (Matthew 5:4–6):

"How blest are the sorrowful;
they shall find consolation.
How blessed are those of a gentle spirit;
they shall have the earth for their possession.
How blest are those who hunger and thirst to see right prevail;
they shall be satisfied."

Typically, however, Jesus turns to the parable. It is not always clear whether he is trying to reach everyone or whether his parables are a way of testing the spiritual readiness of the crowds that followed him. Not everyone was able to decipher his parables. Take, for instance, the parable of the sower (Luke 8:5–8):

"A sower went out to sow his seed. And as he sowed, some seed fell along the footpath, where it was trampled on, and the birds ate it up. Some seed fell on rock and, after coming up, withered for lack of moisture. Some seed fell in among thistles, and the thistles grew up with it and choked it. And some of the seed fell into good soil, and grew, and yielded a hundredfold." As he said this he called out, "If you have ears to hear, then hear."

The disciples are as obtuse as the general public. They turn to Jesus and ask for an interpretation. He prefaces his explanation with mysterious words suggesting that only certain persons can know the secrets of the kingdom of God and that the others will listen to parables but not understand them. The explanation is actually simple enough. It could be summarized by saying that those who have spiritual staying power will show the results of the gospel in their lives.

The parable of the Good Samaritan arose, as many of the parables did, from particular questions addressed to Jesus. The command to love one's neighbor as oneself was already familiar in rabbinical teaching. But the question of how to define neighbor was not so easily settled. The little episode is summarized in Luke 10:25–37:

On one occasion a lawyer came forward to put this test question to him: "Master, what must I do to inherit eternal life?" Jesus said, "What is written in the Law? What is your reading of it?" He replied, "Love the Lord your God with all your heart, with all your soul, with all your strength, and with all your mind; and your neighbour as yourself." "That is the right answer," said Jesus; "do that and you will live."

But he wanted to vindicate himself, so he said to Jesus, "And who is my neighbour?" Jesus replied, "A man was on his way from Jerusalem down to Jericho when he fell in with robbers, who stripped him, beat him, and went off leaving him half dead. It so happened that a priest was going down by the same road; but when he saw him, he went past on the other side. So too a Levite came to the place, and when he saw him went past on the other side. But a Samaritan who was making the journey came upon him, and when he saw him was moved to pity. He went up and bandaged his wounds, bathing them with oil and wine. Then he lifted him on to his own beast, brought him to an inn, and looked after him there. Next day he produced two silver pieces and gave them to the inn-keeper, and said, 'Look after him; and if you spend any more, I will repay you on my way back.' Which of these three do you think was neighbour to the man who fell into the hands of the robbers?" He answered, "The one who showed him kindness," Jesus said, "Go and do as he did."

Through the centuries the voice of the clever lawyer comes down to us, striving to complicate the simple command of love. He wants to know how broad the term is. Jesus might have replied, "Anybody in need, regardless of race, color, creed, or sex is your neighbor." But the words would have been as quickly forgotten as legal briefs in affirmative action cases. To drive home his point, Jesus deliberately chose an extreme case, the Samaritans. They and the Jews of Jerusalem loved each other about as much as the Protestants and Catholics of Northern Ireland. The lawyer is driven to admit that the despised Samaritan (not the priest or the assistant priest) was the true neighbor.

Sometimes the parables are very hard to take. Consider, for instance, the story of the landowner who goes out to hire day-laborers for work in his vineyard. Several times he does this, promising to pay them the usual wage. Then evening falls and it is the time for settling accounts (Matthew 20:8–16):

"When evening fell, the owner of the vineyard said to his steward, 'Call the labourers and give them their pay, beginning with those who came last and ending with the first.' Those who had started work an hour before sunset came forward, and were paid the full day's wage. When it was the turn of the men who had come first they expected something extra, but were paid the same amount as the others. As they took it, they grumbled at their employer: 'These late-comers have done only one hour's work, yet you have put them on a level with us, who have sweated the whole day long in the blazing sun! The owner turned to one of them and said, 'My friend, I am not being unfair to you. You agreed on the usual wage for the day, did you not? Take your pay and go home. I choose to pay the last man the same as you. Surely I am free to do what I like with my own money. Why be jealous because I am kind?' Thus will the last be first, and the first last."

How are we to take this parable? Surely not as a commendation of laissez-faire capitalism. Jesus is not proclaiming a particular style of economic life. Still, the words do offend. It is difficult to imagine any collective bargaining contract that would sanction this system of payment. Surely, if the landowner wants to distribute a bonus he should take into account how many hours each man has worked. But he does not. He stands on his rights. He can spend his money or waste it as he pleases.

This line of reasoning is not getting us far. Perhaps the story points beyond our accustomed ideas of justice. It may be saying there is a realm of existence more profound than everyday work, and in this realm it doesn't greatly matter how many merits a person accumulates. What *does* matter is where he stands when evening falls. He may have awakened to his true nature and needs at the last minute. What counts is the direction he is pointed when darkness descends upon all lives. The drably virtuous may find themselves in the rear of the line. Those who sinned greatly but at the last moment of daylight turned in another direction may find themselves at the head of the procession.

We remember parables because we have to work to understand them. We remember them also because of their wealth of vivid, everyday detail. In a way, they are like the little vignettes from the Book of Proverbs. As we read the parables we see men sowing their crops; thieves attacking a traveler; men standing in a village square hoping for a day's work; a housewife sweeping out her home to find a lost coin; wedding feasts where the wine flows freely. By creating these vivid pictures of ordinary life, Jesus is able to lead the listener beyond the everyday world into a realm that does not cancel out that world but transcends it.

⋙ 10 ⋘

A Stormy Voyage

I have a recurrent fantasy in which I am the chairman of a panel of literary critics. We are interviewing Luke on a high-level TV talk show. "Dr. Luke," I imagine one of my colleagues (or maybe myself) saying, "When you wrote the Book of Acts, what intention did you have? Did you consciously set out to create a work of literary art? Or did you have in mind some extra-literary purpose?"

"I'm afraid I don't understand," Luke finally replies.

Another member of the panel speaks up, "Perhaps we can put it this way: Do you regard your little book as an esthetic construct whose value and power are quite independent of the particular subject or themes contained in it?"

I think Luke's reply would come sooner this time:

"All I wanted to do was tell what happened in the Christian movement after the resurrection and ascension of Christ." I doubt that Luke had ever heard of the doctrine of "art for art's sake." When he set out to write the Book of Acts he had a story—a true story, he insisted—to tell. That was why he took pen in hand. Real communication could never be established between Luke and the nineteenth-century theoreticians of art for art's sake and their more sophisticated and subtle modern descendants.

And yet, that does not quite dispose of the question. Certainly, when Luke put words to paper, he was not in the same frame of mind as a modern novelist who plots the narrative effects of a story he has made up from his imagination. And certainly, Luke accomplished what he intended. Maybe he also accomplished more than his consciously intended. Perhaps he achieved a high level of literary art while aiming only at recounting certain events of first century A.D. history as they actually happened.

This possibility should come as no surprise. The Book of Psalms is not just a hymnal, it is also an anthology of great poetry. The story of King Saul is a magnificent Hebrew epic, comparable in scope and power to the *Iliad*, as well as being a history book. Perhaps C. S. Lewis was right when he flatly stated:*

> ... It is not hard to argue that all the greatest poems have been made by men who valued something else much more than poetry—even if that something else were only cutting down enemies in a cattle-raid or tumbling a girl in bed.

As we have already seen, the Bible can often be read from several vantage points. Take the Book of Acts. It can be enjoyed first of all as literature. Imagine it retitled "The Adventures of a Wandering Missionary." What we have is the biography of a man who, even at the distance of almost two thousand years, seems larger than life but compellingly lifelike. We discover him first in the Middle Eastern world, then on the move from one missionary field to another, and finally in Rome. Adventures, hardships, appalling dangers confront him everywhere. Acts is a biography; it is also a gripping adventure story.

Acts can also be read as a rich trove of information about the world of the eastern Mediterranean, at the time of the Roman Empire's greatest grandeur. A scholar with proper training will readily recognize the fullness of documentation provided for ordinary life: political forces at work, the operations of the courts, the factions into which religious movements are divided, the conditions of travel.

---

* C. S. Lewis, *Rehabilitations and Other Essays* (London: Oxford University Press, 1939), p. 196.

The literary high point of Acts is Paul's adventures and mis-adventures at sea. The background of this is that he is constant-ly being arrested on charges of stirring up disorders by his preaching. The Roman authorities, weary of the whole thing, pass him from hand to hand. Paul finally exercises his right as a Roman citizen, and appeals his case to Caesar. He must there-fore make the perilous trip to Rome.

The story of that unforgettable voyage is told in Acts 27 through 28:15. There seem to be no regular passenger ships available; special arrangements must be made to transport Paul to Italy. The man in charge is the centurion, Julius, who proves to be a kindhearted guard; during one stop he even allows Paul to stay ashore with some friends.

After reaching Myra in Lycia, the conscientious centurion finds a ship bound for Italy and transfers Paul to it. The winds are not favorable. The ship loses much time before it finally ar-rives at a harbor in Crete. The dangerous sailing season is close at hand. Paul is no stranger to dangers, and in the face of perils at sea he begins to display his already tested qualities of leader-ship. He warns the voyagers (Acts 27:10–11*): " 'Men, I can see that our voyage is going to be disastrous and bring great loss to ship and cargo, and to our own lives also,' " But Paul's cautions are brushed aside. Since the harbor is unsuited for wintering, most of the travelers agree that they should put out to sea again, hoping to winter in the Cretan harbor of Phoenix. As they sail along the coast of Crete they are soon assailed by a tempestuous wind, and have to let the ship run before it. The fearful sailors begin to lighten the ship, even throwing over-board its gear. Day after day the storm continues unabated; the landscape is so dark they cannot see the stars or the sun.

Again Paul speaks up, this time with a message of reassur-ance (27:21–25):

> ... Paul stood up before them and said: "Men, you should have tak-en my advice not to sail from Crete; then you would have spared yourselves this damage and loss. But now I urge you to keep up

---

* Biblical quotations in this chapter are from the New International Version.

your courage, because not one of you will be lost; only the ship will be destroyed. Last night an angel of the God whose I am and whom I serve stood beside me and said, 'Do not be afraid, Paul. You must stand trial before Caesar; and God has graciously given you the lives of all who sail with you.' So keep up your courage, men, for I have faith in God that it will happen just as he told me . . ."

The ship has been helpless for two weeks. Now, during the night, they approach land. Twenty fathoms, then fifteen. The sailors try to escape in the ship's boat, but Paul reports this to the centurion, who stops them. With the coming of dawn they are alongside an unknown land. They do, however, notice a sandy shore. The sailors try to beach the ship. It gets caught in crosscurrents and is pounded to pieces. The soldiers want to kill the prisoners to prevent their escape, but the humane centurion intervenes. Some swim to land; others make it to shore clutching planks or fragments of the ship.

They have landed on Malta. The primitive natives are friendly and helpful; they build a bonfire to warm the castaways. Paul is bitten by a viper and the islanders reason he must be a murderer being punished by divine justice. But when he suffers no ill effects, they change their minds. He must be a god. Meanwhile, the chief magistrate of the island invites them to lodge in his dwelling and entertains them for three days. While there, Paul cures the magistrate's father of fever and dysentery, and is soon overwhelmed by multitudes coming to be healed. Eventually they set sail again and arrive in Italy without difficulty. Paul begins his captivity in Rome, awaiting Caesar's pleasure.

In ancient literature there are few equally vivid accounts of travel by sea and catastrophe at sea. The narrative, however, is more than that. It is also a human drama: the fearful sailors concerned only to save their skins, a centurion trying to do his duty as humanely as possible, a strange religious leader sustaining the hopes of pagan crewmen, a chief magistrate living in the thin layer of civilization on the island of Malta, and the natives, scarcely touched by Roman sophistication, but with an instinctive sense of human solidarity.

When Luke wrote this account, he aimed to recount the

story of Paul's voyage to Rome, a turning point in the Nazarene movement. But he was a doctor and an educated man,
with a fine command of literary Greek. Without aiming at artis-
tic effects, he achieved them by being faithful to the actual
events with every literary skill at his command.

⇒ 11 ⇐
Rules and Regulations

The reader who dips into the book of Leviticus quickly experiences a kind of vertigo. The unquestioned assumptions of
ordinary American life are notable by their absence. For instance, the separation of church and state. The average American thinks of his religion as his own private business. If he is a
butcher and uses a set of inaccurate scales, he does not expect to
be imprisoned by the local parson, though he may fear what
could happen if charges were brought against him in the secular courts.

In the Old Testament there is no area of life that is labeled
"secular" and therefore not subject to divine legislation. The
smallest events of ordinary life, the activities that seem farthest
removed from the rapture and terrors of religion, turn out to be
controlled by the same ultimate Lawgiver as are the details of
worship and the basic decrees of morality. The Old Testament
ideal is theocratic. The ultimate ruler is not president or king,
but he who brought the world into existence and labored pa-
tiently to instill in one particular people the way they should
live day by day, minute by minute.

The result is that Leviticus seems at first a helter-skelter of
precepts varying from moral admonitions to cultic practices to
what an anthropologist would classify as a highly developed
tabu system. From the Old Testament viewpoint, it is all a

seamless fabric; from the secularized view of post-medieval Christianity, it is a strange mixture of the "sacred" and the "secular," tossed into the same book without any very clear arrangement.

The mention of post-medieval Christianity reminds us that Christian cultures have not always made the sharp distinction between the sacred and the secular, church and state, that prevails today in most of the western world. During the Middle Ages, a man might find himself fined for failing to attend church, or disciplined for lending money at interest (usury). Ecclesiastical courts sometimes operated parallel to the secular courts. As late as the Pilgrims who came to the New World, the idea of the holy and unified society was still strong. Only gradually did religion come to be the private activity of people who responded to its appeal.

The rules and regulations spelled out in Leviticus and elsewhere served, in many cases, an obviously practical purpose. Examples are the injunctions against murder, theft, adultery, and the like, as well as the detailed provisions stipulating how the poor should be aided, inheritances regulated, and family continuity assured. But we are talking in modern categories. The ancient Hebrews, responding to the messages entrusted to Moses, believed that the ultimate goal of the individual and his society was holiness. This was to be attained by obedience to *all* the divine commandments and prohibitions. The Mosaic Law specified in the most minute detail how the Holy One should be hallowed by a particular pattern of life. And as he was hallowed, simultaneously society was made holy.

Certainly, Leviticus contains provision after provision that a modern reader will regard as neither practical legislation for everyday life, nor as manifestations of religion. It is interesting to pick out a section a page or two in length, and see if one can classify the precepts in categories such as legal code, moral precepts, tabus, and modes of worship. For example, chapter 19 sets a particular tone from the beginning, with the emphasis on holiness: " 'Be holy, for I, Yahweh, your God, am holy.' " * This

---

*Biblical quotations in this chapter are from the Jerusalem Bible.

leads to a bit of moral instruction, " 'Each of you must respect his father and mother,' " which is evidently seen as an aspect of holiness. Soon thereafter idols are denounced, followed by a cultic provision regulating the offering of sacrifices. Abruptly the holy voice shifts emphasis, and speaks of provision for the poor, assigning them the gleanings of the harvest. The principles of basic morality dominate the chapter from now on. The necessary prohibitions that any society must have—not to steal, not to defraud your neighbor—are stated, one after the other. Examples of forbidden conduct are given: holding back a worker's wages until the following morning, cursing the dumb, tripping a blind person.

Contrary to the widespread impression that the Old Testament deals with external conduct and is indifferent to states of mind, this chapter also forbids concealed hatred for one's neighbor, and in words later to become more familiar, commands: "You must love your neighbor as yourself."

At this point the passage abruptly turns to the kind of items our imaginary anthropologist would rejoice to discover: two different kinds of cattle must not be mated; a person must not wear clothing made with two sorts of fabric. Then as abruptly there is legislation against sleeping with another man's concubine. Now comes a welter of other prohibitions: don't eat anything with blood in it; don't trim the edges of your beard; don't tattoo yourself; don't turn your daughter into a prostitute; stay away from mediums; stand in the presence of gray-haired people; love the foreigner in your midst as though he were a native; use honest weights and measures. The sanction for all these assorted prohibitions and commands is the same: "I am Yahweh."

For another example of the infinitely detailed concerns of Leviticus, consider chapter 5. Here there is the same mixture of cult, morality, and custom, with the emphasis this time strongly on morality, in particular how a person can be purified after violating one of the prohibitions. First comes a list of sins: keeping quiet when one should give evidence at a trial; touching the dead body of an unclean animal; contact with human uncleanness, taking an oath and then disregarding it. Detailed directions are given for restoring the offender to ritual purity. He must confess his deed and bring a sheep or goat as a sacrifice. If he cannot afford so expensive an offering, two pigeons will do. If the pigeons are beyond his pocketbook he can substitute a small quantity of flour. This is one of the many instances in the Old Testament of a kind of sociological realism— a recognition, built into law, that some are rich and some are poor.

The passage then moves to additional divine legislation governing social relations. Note that this is still within the context of the will of Yahweh (5:20–26):

> Yahweh spoke to Moses; he said:
> "If anyone sins and is guilty of fraud against Yahweh by deceiving his neighbour over a deposit or a security, or by withholding something due to him or exploiting him;
> "or if he finds lost property and denies it;
> "or if he perjures himself about any sin that a man may commit;
> "if he sins and so becomes answerable, he is to restore what he has taken or demanded in excess: the deposit confided to him, the lost property that he found, or any object about which he has perjured himself. He must add one-fifth to the principal and pay the whole to whoever held the property rights on the day when he became answerable. Then he is to bring an unblemished ram of his flock to Yahweh as a sacrifice of reparation: it must be valued according to the rate paid to the priest for a sacrifice of reparation. The priest shall perform the rite of atonement over him before Yahweh and he will be forgiven, whatever the act for which he became answerable."

The American reader, coming perhaps from a secularized suburb and relegating religion to an optional corner of private life, may well feel hurled into a world he never bargained for. Seeking analogies, he may think of Confucionist China with its network of sacred customs and ceremonies. Certainly, he is not in the world of modern-style individualism. Personal conduct is viewed in the light of social relations, and everything is viewed in the light of the mysterious will that pervades the world and has things to say about daily morality, expiation of sin, beard styles, and the cattle breeding industry. A sense of suffocation may be the first reaction—Big Brother is watching me.

And there we will leave it for the moment. Such a reaction is natural to a modern, sophisticated American. It was not the reaction of the people to whom this way of life was first proclaimed. They saw it not as prison but as liberation.

⇒ 12 ⇐

A Runaway Slave

One literary genre poorly represented in the Bible is the personal letter. Indeed, there is only one—the letter that Paul wrote to Philemon. It is unlike all of Paul's other letters, which typically deal with theological questions or problems of church life. In Philemon he is writing to ask a personal favor. The letter is short enough to quote in full*:

Paul, a prisoner of Christ Jesus, and Timothy our brother,

To Philemon our dear friend and fellow worker, to Apphia our sister, to Archippus our fellow soldier and to the church that meets in your home:

Grace to you and peace from God our Father and the Lord Jesus Christ.

I always thank my God as I remember you in my prayers, because I hear about your faith in the Lord Jesus and your love for all the saints. I pray that you may be active in sharing your faith, so that you will have a full understanding of every good thing we have in Christ. Your love has given me great joy and encouragement, because you, brother, have refreshed the hearts of the saints.

Therefore, although in Christ I could be bold and order you to do what you ought to do, yet I appeal to you on the basis of love. I

---

* This quotation is from the New International Version.

then, as Paul—an old man and now also a prisoner of Christ Jesus—I appeal to you for my son Onesimus, who became my son
while I was in chains. Formerly he was useless to you, but now he
has become useful both to you and to me.

I am sending him—who is my very heart—back to you. I would
have liked to keep him with me so that he could take your place in
helping me while I am in chains for the gospel. But I did not want
to do anything without your consent, so that any favor you do will
be spontaneous and not forced. Perhaps the reason he was separat-
ed from you for a little while was that you might have him back for
good—no longer as a slave, but better than a slave, as a dear brother. He is very dear to me but even dearer to you, both as a man and
as a brother in the Lord.

So if you consider me a partner, welcome him as you would welcome me. If he has done you any wrong or owes you anything,
charge it to me. I, Paul, am writing this with my own hand. I will
pay it back—not to mention that you owe me your very self. I do
wish, brother, that I may have some benefit from you in the Lord;
refresh my heart in Christ. Confident of your obedience, I write to
you, knowing that you will do even more than I ask.

And one thing more: Prepare a guest room for me, because I
hope to be restored to you in answer to your prayers.

Epaphras, my fellow prisoner for Christ Jesus, sends you greetings. And so do Mark, Aristarchus, Demas and Luke, my fellow
workers.

The grace of the Lord Jesus Christ be with your spirit.

Clearly this is a letter to a close personal friend. Philemon
was one of Paul's converts and the church in Colossae (near
Ephesus) met in his large home. Onesimus was a slave who had
run away from Philemon, probably with some stolen travel
money in his pocket. He turns up in Rome, that great Mecca of
runaways who hope to disappear into the anonymous crowds
of the teeming city. Somehow he meets Paul, who is living under house arrest, awaiting his hearing before Caesar. Influenced by Paul, he becomes a Christian.

The great missionary is confronted by a delicate problem.
He has always taught that one should obey the laws of the
state, and here is a runaway slave clearly violating the law. At
the same time Paul wants to make sure that if he does send the

slave back to his master, he will be kindly received. Such is his dilemma as he sits down to write a letter which Onesimus can take with him and show to Philemon. All Paul's persuasive skills are called into action. He chooses to woo Philemon's cooperation rather than command it.

The letter is a marvel of rhetorical persuasion. First, a gradual beginning. Paul praises Philemon for all he has done to encourage the church in Colossae, and describes the deep pleasure he had experienced from knowing Philemon: "Your love has given me great joy and encouragement, because you, brother, have refreshed the hearts of the saints."

By this time, the personal relation of Paul and Philemon has been movingly expressed, and the word love has been introduced as the theme of the letter. Paul briefly considers the possibility of an outright command but rejects it. Philemon must make his own decision, but—and this is crucial—it must be a decision consonant with love: "Therefore, although in Christ I could be bold and order you to do what you ought to do, yet I appeal to you on the basis of love." This is a skillfully double-edged sentence, at once saying what decision the master should make, and at the same time refraining from any categorical command that he make it.

Almost in a parenthesis, Paul mentions his captivity in Rome. How can Philemon refuse his old friend in these circumstances? But again, Paul is careful not to come on too strong. He even inserts a pun on Onesimus' name, which literally means "useful." Thus he maintains the relaxed tone of the letter while being deeply in earnest. He smoothly avoids provoking a defensive reaction.

Apparently the runaway slave has done little chores for Paul, and the latter would like to keep him. But Paul makes it clear that he respects the master's right of decision: he will not spiritually coerce him into a particular course of action. Still, he hopes that if the slave, now a Christian, returns to Philemon, their new relation as brothers in the faith will inspire Philemon not only to forgive the slave but perhaps to grant his freedom. Paul now draws upon the accumulated good will and gratitude that Philemon feels for him: "So if you consider me a

partner, welcome him as you would welcome me." If the slave
has stolen anything, Paul will replace it. Then in the middle of
a sentence he recalls the debt (conversion) that Philemon owes
him: "You owe me your very self." And finally, in a command
not phrased as a command, he says, "I write to you, knowing
that you will do even more than I ask." The plea ends abruptly
at this point. The rest is up to Philemon.

The letter is indeed a marvel of persuasion, never intruding
on the autonomy of Philemon's decisions, but arousing all his
best instincts and drawing strength from the close relation of
friendship the two men enjoy. There is no record of Philemon's
welcome to the returning slave, but if it had been harsh it
seems unlikely that this little letter would have found its way
into the New Testament.

Not until modern times did it become a frequent practice to
publish the private letters of famous men and women. In these
one often finds new insights into their inner thoughts and
feelings, the private face behind the public mask. For this reason, the letter to Philemon is a precious sidelight on that
towering figure of antiquity, Paul. Usually we see him standing up to all the perils of existence, wholly dedicated to his
work as a missionary. One would think such a man would have
no time to worry about an unimportant slave who had foolish-
ly run away from his master. But Paul, as we see from this letter, was not a person involved only in the great moments and
movements of history. He was also one who could be concerned about Tom, Dick, and Harry, as well as this church and
that church. He differs sharply from many of the giant figures
of history who have loved humanity with indiscriminate dedication, but never found time to forge a bond with any individual. Paul may at times seem a stern, even a forbidding figure.
He could be implacable when he was convinced he needed to
be. But he had time to spare and ears to listen when a young
slave stumbled into his life.

Part Two

A

SECOND
LOOK

❧ 13 ❧

The X-Dimension

In writing a poem, I sometimes have a strange experience. I set out with great confidence. I *think* I have a clear idea of the poem's theme. My job is to handle all the technicalities: determine the metrical form, create whatever metaphors I want to use, control the length of the poem. And for a time all goes well. The poem, as I compose it line by line, is obedient to my will. I am the master.

After a while I have an odd feeling. It is as though an invisible hand were resting on my right hand, trying to guide it. It wants me to write words and lines I have not planned. Some nameless force, some anonymous intelligence is trying to change the course of the poem. At this point I can get my back up, and I sometimes do. I decide to fight it out. And I may win the conflict, by sheer determination. Exhausted but triumphant, I put the finished poem aside, and only after some weeks come back to have a last look at it before mailing it out for publication. And at that moment, the battle between me and the mysterious force trying to guide my hand is renewed. I find that the poem sounds forced. I can detect the exact line in which the struggle with the alien intelligence began. The remainder of the poem has an unnatural air about it, as though it had been beaten and twisted into shape. I see now I should have relaxed and allowed the mysterious second poet to take over. He knew better than I what the poem on its deepest level was trying to say.

When I began this book, I was determined to let the Bible

speak with its multiple voices. I did not presuppose that the reader brought with him any particular interest in religion; I wanted to show him the treasures he would find if he read the Bible as though it were a book he just happened to pick up from a shelf. And I think I have succeeded. In our preliminary explorations we have encountered masterpieces of literature, and passages or whole books that would fascinate the historian, sociologist, or anthropologist. I treated the Bible as an anthology of ancient literature, and such in fact it is.

But the question I deliberately bypassed was whether there is one overall something-or-other that makes the Bible one book as well as many books. Is there a theme or insight that unites the most diverse books of the Bible? Gradually I began to feel the mysterious guiding hand on my hand. It seemed to have things it wanted me to say. What it did was drive me to think about whatever it is that gives the Bible a unity transcending its diversity.

Let me turn now to a couple of analogies. If you are walking through the woods, you may gradually become aware of a particular fragrance. Perhaps the source is some locust trees with their white blossoms and haunting perfume. You may not ever come on the actual trees, but you are enveloped by their presence. Your feelings and thoughts, so to speak, begin to be perfumed; the unseen trees bear witness of their reality by the fragrance they send you.

Or take another analogy. I am sitting in my study on a small Vermont lake. From across the lake comes the music of a composition by Vivaldi. Until this moment I was not consciously aware of it. But now I suddenly recognize that the music has gained entrance into my mind. It is subtly altering the sentences that I write. The very rhythms of this prose that you are reading show the shaping influence of the musical phrases that quietly reach me as a gift of the unseen record player across the lake.

I have just reread the earlier part of this book, and have found a pervasive fragrance, a persistent music that I did not deliberately put there. In places where I was most consciously writing of the literary, historical, sociological, and anthropo-

logical dimensions of the Bible, I was haunted by rumors of realities that go beyond any of the above.

One final analogy may help. Years ago a British mathemati-
cian and theologian, Edwin A. Abbott, wrote a book called *Flat-
lands*. In it he describes a world with only two dimensions.
There is no height. Disturbing rumors of a third dimension
sometimes penetrate this world, but its inhabitants cannot
imagine such metaphysical speculations. And yet, even if the
poor Flatlanders cannot conceive it, the third dimension *does*
exist.

We are better off than the Flatlanders. We begin with a
three-dimensional world—length, breadth, and height. But the
words of the Bible come to us with rumors of a fourth dimension. It is not a dimension that can be measured with a ruler. It
is more a fragrance in the woods or mysterious music invisibly,
but audibly coming from across the lake.

As we continue reading the Bible, we find the fragrance, the
music, the fourth dimension everywhere. It is as much present
in rules and regulations for commercial transactions as in those
high moments when there is a hint of ultimate mysteries. At
this point the reader may ask impatiently, "Why play these
word games? The language of the Bible is clear enough." Indeed, scarcely a page occurs without such words as Lord, Yahweh, or God. Why seek new words or analogies, when these
words already exist and are universally—more or less—understood?

The "more or less" is the catch. Even the person who has
never read the Bible brings to it whatever concepts of the divine he has picked up from conversations and literary allu-
sions. The trouble is that the concepts that popularly go with
these familiar words are usually too simple for the reality that I
propose to call, for lack of any better term, the X-Dimension.*
For example, "the Father Almighty" suggests an aged but vig-
orous man with a long white beard, and by itself has clear over-

---

*After I had settled on this term, I came on Erich Fromm's book *You Shall Be as
Gods* (New York: Holt, Rinehart & Winston, 1966) and was interested to find
that he uses the symbol of the unknown quantity, x, in a similar way. Perhaps
this metaphor is not altogether arbitrary.

tones of male chauvinism. There is no balancing phrase such as
Mother Almighty. To think of God as being like the best conceivable father is not totally wrong, but is inadequate to suggest the full reality.

Other readers, influenced by the Greek philosophy that is
part of the air we breathe, think of the Divine in terms of "the
unmoved mover." The unmoved mover is more a principle of
mathematics than a Being with whom one can enter into a
transforming relation. This concept again is not totally wrong,
but it says little about the God of Abraham, Isaac, and Jacob.

Still other readers find the X-Dimension in the still voice
within. Again, not wrong but inadequate. In the Bible the divine voice speaks in multiple ways: sometimes to a whole people, but often to the solitary individual when he explores the
deepest level of his being. The X-Dimension is certainly that.
But it is more than that.

The advantage of temporarily choosing a term without prior
content is that we avoid presuppositions, and let the content
gradually be filled in as we explore the Bible further. Bit by bit,
intuition by intuition, our makeshift phrase can take on concreteness and meaning. And eventually we shall be able to
push it aside, like scaffolding no longer needed, and learn to
use the simple word, God, without committing ourselves to a
big man with a white beard or an elegant mathematical formu-
la.

So, for the moment, X-Dimension it is—a way of bringing
together the fragrance of locust trees, the sound of Vivaldi
borne on the breeze across the lake, the irruption of verticality
into a flat universe.

14
Return Visits

I propose now to pay brief return visits to certain portions of the Bible that we examined earlier. The object this time is not to find literature and sociology, but to discover evidences of the X-Dimension.

Dipping at random into the Book of Proverbs, I encounter such short sayings as (14:31*):

He who oppresses the poor insults his Maker;
he who is generous to the needy honours him.

A few lines farther down, I come on this (15:3):

The eyes of the Lord are everywhere,
surveying evil and good men alike.

Evidently, morality is not merely a series of negative commands—don't kill, don't commit adultery, and so forth. It is also—and more importantly—positive obligations, like relieving the wants of the poor. And watching over the human scene are the divine eyes, passing judgment on the deeds of mankind. Offering sacrifices in the Temple is one form of worship; the Book of Proverbs implies that an equally important form is ordinary morality and societal obligations. Both are a form of obedience to the will of the mysterious X-Dimension.

Where does this leave the "secular world"? That's rather like asking where the canary is, after the cat has come into the room. There is still the perfectly familiar world of our daily decisions, triumphs, and failures, but the standards by which we are judged are not a Gallup Poll consensus. These standards come from above. The way I behave toward my neighbor is a revelation of my attitude toward the divine source of moral

---

* Biblical quotations in this chapter are from the New English Bible, unless otherwise indicated.

standards. He does not need to check up on me at the Temple to see whether I am taking a proper part in specifically "religious" activities; all he needs to do is check the accuracy of my scales.

If the X-Dimension ranks the objects of its supervision from 1 to 10, it is not on the basis of rarified mystical raptures or even consent to the mysteries of theology. The Dimension is much more down-to-earth than that. It watches what we do, the Book of Proverbs says, and our actions speak louder than our words. By aiding the poor, dealing honestly with our fellows, and using rather than abusing our sexual instincts, we hallow our lives and acknowledge the ultimate holiness of the one who has revealed the way of life he wants us to follow. Temple or marketplace, the setting makes no difference.

One of the main reasons the Book of Psalms is enduring poetry is the vision of nature that it so vividly expresses. The physical universe of land and sea and trees and beasts and people is not dismissed as a meaningless or illusory phenomenon. It simply *is*. And there is no poetry that proclaims this *isness*, this utter reality, with more power.

But the ancient Hebrew authors of the Psalms were not content to leave it at that. The universe was real because the X-Dimension is more real. There is an intelligent power that willed the universe into existence and sustains its reality day by day. The universe is real because that power is more real.

Just as in the Book of Proverbs we see everyday society as the stage on which we act out our relation with whatever is ultimate, so in the Psalms we see ourselves as solid, physical beings, in a world whose every detail is equally solid. It is no wonder that the great achievements of science have been mostly in countries whose religion teaches that the world we see with eyes and explore with microscopes and telescopes shares some of the solidness of the creator. A scientist can hope that his discoveries are really valid, for the universe itself is not an illusion.

One major function of the Psalms was to tell the story of the Hebrew people and to internalize it, so that all their experience would be seen in the light of the early and shaping events of their national history. An example is Psalm 78:12–16 (KJV), describing the exodus from Egypt:

> Marvellous things did he in the sight of their fathers, in the land of Egypt, in the field of Zoan. He divided the sea, and caused them to pass through; and he made the waters to stand as an heap. In the daytime also he led them with a cloud, and all the night with a light of fire. He clave the rocks in the wilderness, and gave them drink as out of the great depths. He brought streams also out of the rock, and caused waters to run down like rivers.

This psalm goes on to detail the rebellious attitude of the people toward the Lord, and then describes the escape from Egypt in language so vivid that it must have become embedded in the heart and soul of anyone joining with his fellows in singing the history of his people. And that, one might argue, is the main religious function of the Psalms. They express, in memorable language, the understanding the Hebrews had of their own special history.

The very qualities that made the Book of Ecclesiastes suspect when it first began to circulate help to explain why it speaks so powerfully more than two thousand years later. It offers no easy answers. It is not the peal of a trumpet, proclaiming that good will be rewarded and evil be punished, in this life or the next. It has no easy certainties to offer. Life is simply what it is, a mix of good and bad, growth and decay, and has to be accepted as it is. The one certain destination is physical ruin and death. Meanwhile, we must live day by day with modest hopes in the time remaining (Ecclesiastes 12:6, RSV): "Before the silver cord is snapped, or the golden bowl is broken, or the pitcher is broken at the fountain, or the wheel broken at the cistern. . . ."

But the certainty of death is not the final desolation. The ultimate emptiness is the sad recognition that the accounts are never brought into balance. Neither in this life nor any life beyond (if there is one) are the good certain to be rewarded and the evil punished. The X-Dimension does not have a refrigerator in which lollypops are stored for good boys and girls. If the

Preacher is to live the kind of life that the divine Lawmaker has decreed, it cannot be as part of a contract. He must do good simply because it is good, not because it will pay off. Thus in the Book of Ecclesiastes the focus shifts sharply to the lonely, bewildered individual, trying to thread his way through life as the gradual approach of evening and darkness warn him that life in the flesh is moving toward disintegration, with the great questions still unanswered.

The ethical nobility of the Preacher consists precisely in this: he refuses to deceive himself by pretending that the world has a rationality which he has not been able to discern. But he does not leave it at that. He chooses good not because it will be rewarded, but simply because it *is* good. One senses that if he even lost all belief in a cosmic lawmaker, he would not change his way of life. He is a human being, endowed with the unique traits that go with that status, and—God or no God—he will live according to his vision of right and wrong.

And here perhaps is the clue to the inclusion of Ecclesiastes in the canon of the Bible. One can live a righteous life because the neighbors expect it, or because the invisible Lawmaker does. But one can also live it simply because it is right. The Preacher might not know what is in the grave and beyond; he might not understand why the wicked so often prosper and the innocent suffer. But even if God did not exist, the Preacher would live as though he did.

We read the Book of Ruth as one of the world's great short stories, and so indeed it is. But it was written first of all as a story with a message. There are several clues to this. One is the Hebrew fondness for names with significant meaning. Naomi's sons are named "sickness" and "pining away," and Ruth probably means "the beloved." These names suggest that some kind of moralizing tale is about to be narrated.

A second clue is the little genealogical summary at the end of the story, where we learn that Boaz (and Ruth) were the parents of Obed, who was the father of Jesse, who was the father of David. And David, no Hebrew needed be reminded, was the great king whose life and reign foreshadowed the Messiah promised to the Hebrew people. At this point a Christian reader goes further, and recalls that Jesus was of Davidic lineage, and that therefore one of his ancestors was a gentile.

This preoccupation with genealogy may seem tiresome to a modern reader. But vital questions were at stake. The question that constantly had to be faced by the Chosen People was that of interfaith marriage. Did it pose a threat not merely to the ethnic integrity of the Hebrews, but also to their relation with the one with whom they had made a special covenant? The question came to a head when a group of Hebrews returned to Jerusalem from Babylon and found that many of the people who had stayed in the holy city had intermarried with pagans and were being rapidly assimilated. Ezra, the leader of the return, was horrified to find how far this process had gone (Ezra, chapters 9 and 10). He tore his garments and fell into a stupor of horror. He forbade mixed marriages and insisted that those already in existence should be dissolved.

Ezra's drastic measures did not quite settle the question. It was still being debated several centuries later, at the time when the story of Ruth was composed. Thus what we have in Ruth is a counterblast to the long deceased Ezra and his followers. Ruth is everything one would wish to have in a daughter. She is a good wife; she accepts the religion of the Hebrew family into which she marries. When afflictions come thick and fast upon the exiles, she shares their hardships. Who could honestly argue that she was a threat to the integrity and religious heritage of the Hebrew people? Indeed, the implication is quite clear that she became a more exemplary Hebrew than most of those who took their status for granted.

All these things do not mean that Ruth is not a magnificent short story. But it is more than that. It is a powerful statement of one viewpoint: that the doors of the Hebrew covenant are wide open to all who knock and wish to enter.

At this point, the invisible hand that wants to guide my writing is edging me away from the X-Dimension and pointing with increasing frequency toward the monosyllable God, and other terms such as the Lord and Yahweh. As I pay a return visit to the story of King Saul, my stopgap name for the mysterious and numinous presence that impinges upon us does not seem strong or focused enough to express what the Bible is trying to say.

It is essential to bear in mind that this story, as we have it, is *interpreted* history. The ancient events are narrated from the viewpoint of the prophets, who were profoundly suspicious of all earthly kings. Samuel, who reluctantly anointed Saul as king, fully shared these misgivings, and was quick to turn against Saul when the latter disobeyed the voice of God as that voice was mediated through the revelations of Samuel.

What Saul could never achieve was simple, unquestioning obedience. In complex situations he insisted on thinking for himself, and thus incurred the wrath of God, who had already given him his specific marching orders. From a purely human viewpoint, we may sometimes find more nobility of soul in Saul than in his tormenter, the prophet Samuel—but that is not the way the author or editor of this book saw it. The theme is obedience, and Saul was repeatedly disobedient to the lord of the universe.

From a humanistic viewpoint the story of Saul is a smear job, like Shakespeare's *Richard III,* which blackens the house of York and glorifies the triumphant Tudors. But the narrator of Saul's sorrows would doubtless have brushed aside such compassionate thoughts. Saul had his chance; he failed through lack of unquestioning obedience, and one better than he (David), who had been waiting in the wings, moved out to stage center.

The Song of Songs is a collection of poetry glorifying nuptial love. But once the collection was in existence it was inevitable that readers should begin finding in it additional levels of meaning. The human imagination is incurably metaphorical. Throughout the Bible there is the intuition that the relation between the individual and God is the most intense one possible. Now comes the Song of Songs depicting the most profound relation that human beings can have with each other. It was not a great leap to see in this poetry a celebration of the relation between God and the nation or the individual.

The prophet Hosea had already set the pattern, centuries earlier, when he likened God to a loving and forgiving bridegroom, and Israel to a faithless—but still loved—wife. Subsequent to Hosea, other prophets used the same metaphor. For example, we find Isaiah saying in 50:1–2:

> The LORD says,
> Is there anywhere a deed of divorce
> by which I have put your mother away?
> Was there some creditor of mine
> to whom I sold you?
> No; it was through your own wickedness that you were sold
> and for your own misconduct that your mother was put away.
> Why, then, did I find no one when I came?
> Why, when I called, did no one answer?
> Did you think my arm too short to redeem,
> did you think I had no power to save?

Later we find Jeremiah proclaiming in 2:1–2:

> The word of the LORD came to me: Go, make a proclamation that all Jerusalem shall hear: These are the words of the LORD:
>
> > I remember the unfailing devotion of your youth,
> > the love of your bridal days,
> > when you followed me in the wilderness,
> > through a land unsown.

All this begins to explain why the Song of Songs was retained in the Bible. Written long after the time of the major prophets, it was inevitably read in the light of their teachings. A basic part of the prophetic message was the role of the Hebrew nation as the bride of God. By this comparison, all the modulations of love, fidelity, unfaithfulness, exile and return, repentence, and forgiveness could be expressed through one complex metaphor.

But it is part of the richness of the Bible that no one analogy is adequate for God. Another symbol, frequently used, is that of fatherhood. God as King of Kings is also frequently employed throughout the Bible, evoking visions of the splendor of earthly monarchs infinitely magnified. The advantage of multiple symbols is that all of them together suggest a better balanced vision of the Ultimate than any symbol alone could do.

Given the metaphorical mode of expression found in the Bible from beginning to end, it was natural and perhaps inevitable that these exquisite poems, celebrating the joys of marriage, should quickly become symbols of something more: the love of God for Israel, and eventually the relation of Christ and the Church or Christ and the individual.

But a last word. These poems of human love remain poems of human love. The metaphorical meanings are there, but the literal meanings are not erased. Through the centuries, the Song of Songs continues to celebrate the splendor of human love, as well as the love freely offered to mankind by the author of the universe.

It would be possible to revisit the six remaining portions of the Bible that we examined earlier, but it hardly seems necessary. We have found that the central figure is what I for a time called the X-Dimension and now simply call God. In one way or another he is shown at work everywhere in the Bible. And his presence is the explanation of the fragrance of the locust trees, the sound of distant music, and the stealthy invasion of our lives by the fourth dimension. There is no place to hide. And no reason for choosing to hide.

Part Three

❧ THE ❧
FIVE-ACT
DRAMA

✣ 15 ✣

Recurrent Themes

We started out to read the Bible as we would any other book. This approach carried us a considerable distance, but ultimately proved inadequate. As we dug trial excavations in the vast terrain of the Bible, we became aware of a pressure from somewhere. Something in addition to literature or social studies was demanding attention.

True, the Bible is literature—great literature. But its central theme is the activity of the mysterious power which in the Bible goes by many names: Yahweh, the Lord, the Father Almighty, God. We were driven to reread some of the passages we had examined earlier, and in every case we found the X-Dimension clamoring to be heard. Our main quest from now on will be to discern how God reveals himself as the primary reality in the Bible.

But before attempting that, we might ask what we have so far deduced about the Biblical perspective. And at this point you may well wonder why so little has been said about the New Testament. The first reason is simply that the Old Testament is more than three times longer than the New. That is roughly the ratio maintained in our explorations. The second reason is that Christians and agnostics alike have a woeful tendency to concentrate so heavily on the New Testament that they skim all too lightly over the Old Testament. Difficult as the latter is for the reader who is approaching it for the first time, some familiarity with the Old Testament is essential if one is to understand the rise and development of the Jewish sect that evolved into Christianity.

At this point we come to an inescapable dilemma. Jews and Christians simply do not interpret the Old Testament in the same way when they ask themselves how Jesus fits into the total picture. The Christian sees in Jesus the fulfillment of the messianic prophecies; the Jew believes the Messiah is yet to come. The path in the wood forks, and one must travel one way or the other. Writing as a Christian, I inevitably read the Old Testament in New Testament categories.

Meanwhile, it is possible to list a number of biblical themes that run through both testaments. Some have already received passing attention; others will figure in subsequent chapters.

One theme is that the universe is something that came into existence through the will of God. He told it to be, and it was. It bears the same relation to God that a painting does to the artist that painted it. The painting reveals the artist by the mere fact of its existence but it is not the artist. However, this analogy breaks down if pushed too far. When the artist finishes a painting and hangs it on the wall, that is that. God not merely creates a universe; he sustains it. It is a continuing and dynamic process, as though the painting on the wall were constantly being revised and updated by the artist.

The creative process is not confined to God. We, made in his image, are his junior partners, challenged to exercise our stewardship over the earth entrusted to us, and inspired to create new things—poems, paintings, symphony orchestras, legal systems, methods of agriculture and industry—to complete the fullness of the earth.

Since the physical universe is the result of God's will, it follows that the biblical perspective is life-affirming. It rejoices in the solidity of this world. A good meal is a sacrament of the goodness of creation; the love of husband and wife proclaims the vitalities of God's world. If there is something wrong in our relation with the senior creator, it is not going to be cured by pretending we are disembodied angels.

One of the Bible's most profound insights is also a very simple one: that God and morality are inseparably linked. The Judeo-Christian God demands not merely reverence but also obedience to the moral law that in various ways he has proclaimed.

But surely, the reader will say, all religions have this understanding. They do not. The Greeks with their brawling and conniving Olympic gods did not count upon their deities to teach them morality; they turned instead to the philosophers. The ancient pagan cults with their sacred prostitution and human sacrifices were also dubious examples of the combination of religion and morality. It is the glory of the ancient Hebrews that to them it was first clearly revealed that worship of God and daily morality are two sides of one coin.

Indeed, as we have seen, the distinction between "sacred" and "secular" soon breaks down. Leaving some grain on the ground for poor gleaners is as much a religious deed as offering animals for ritual sacrifice. Explicitly "religious" moments, as in the great ceremonies in the Temple, might be the high points, but their ultimate validity was confirmed or negated by daily life. Either everything in life is hallowed or nothing is.

One striking thing about the Bible is its unrelentingly realistic view of human nature. It sees man as established in his dignity by the image he bears within him; it also sees him as a rebel, defying the very God that created him. The Bible is implacably the foe of all reductionist theories—"man is nothing but a biological mechanism." At the same time, it recognizes the demonic potentialities in everyone. In its view of human nature, the Bible strikes a delicate balance between naive idealism and dour pessimism. There are few greater figures in the Old Testament than David, the prototype of the hoped for Messiah, and yet the Bible makes no attempt to give a glossily perfect portrait of him. He was in many ways an ideal king, but also capable of having one of his soldiers killed so he could sleep with a woman whom his wandering eyes had discovered. Peter, who did so much to establish the Christian faith outside of Palestine, was also a craven coward. No official portrait painter would include these blemishes on the noble faces, but the Bible does.

The Bible asserts that, beginning with the "fall" of Adam and Eve, mankind is alienated from its creator. If that gap is to be bridged, the initiative must be taken by the creator himself. The Old Testament pins its main hopes on obedience to the Law, or on the coming of God's anointed, the Messiah, who will bring a new order of existence into being. In the New Testament, the hopes are focused on Christ. In God's good time, both Testaments promise, our alienation will be healed as God acts in one way or another to heal it.

One very important pair of themes in the Bible is Covenant and Chosen People. A covenant is simply a formal agreement between humankind and its creator. Man promises to live according to the commands of God. God promises his protection and help in time of need. It is a contract, witnessed by all of creation.

At least one covenant embraces mankind as a whole. This is when, after the great deluge, Yahweh promises never again to destroy humanity by a flood; the sign is the rainbow. A specifically Hebrew covenant is found in Abraham's obedience to the Lord, with circumcision as the symbol of God's promises to the Hebrew people. The climactic Old Testament covenant is the one at Sinai. The people promise to worship Yahweh alone and obey his moral and cultic decrees, and he promises to bring them safely into the Promised Land.

With the passage of time, the prophets discerned also a more inward kind of covenant, written in the heart rather than publicly proclaimed. It needed no physical token. Finally, Christians saw in Christ's institution of Holy Communion a new testament or covenant (I Corinthians 11:25, KJV): "After the same manner also he took the cup, when he had supped, saying, 'This cup is the new testament in my blood: this do ye, as often as ye drink it, in remembrance of me.' " At this moment, the doors of all the covenants open wide.

But back to Old Testament times. With the idea of covenants went the concept of "Chosen People." It is perhaps the central theme of the Old Testament—and is likely to be distasteful when first encountered. Why should God play favorites? If the Hebrews were his chosen people, were the ancient Greeks and Chinese second-class souls? Fair or unfair, there the concept is, squarely planted in the Old Testament. There is hope held out that all human beings will one day enter upon their own covenant with God; meanwhile, he seems to devote most of his attention to one small nation.

True. But if the relation was a special one and the promises were heady, the demands made on the Hebrews were terrifying. The nation was like a soldier called out of line by the sergeant and instructed to search a jungle from which no one has previously returned alive. A high honor but a frightening one. The lone soldier, venturing into the jungle of the unknown, *may* bring back tidings of value not merely to his own army but to all men and women who seek some ultimate revelation. Or he may not come back.

☙ 16 ☙

The Freedom of the Actors

At this point, we have our choice between several approaches to the Bible. We could, of course, continue digging random postholes and come up with many literary, historical, and anthropological items, as well as religious insights. This would not be a false approach to the Bible, but it would ultimately prove too limited. It would not give us one unifying concept of what the total Bible is saying. We would continue to experience the Bible as an anthology of fragments, rather than one book.

Another approach is to read the Bible to find "What it says to *me*." This also is a fruitful approach. The Alone does indeed speak to the alone. A man shipwrecked on a desert isle might well read the Bible in this way, and it would not be a mistake. He would have no opportunity to obey the commands that presuppose a human population of more than one, but he could learn what his relation to God ought to be.

But what would be the only possible approach for the castaway on his desert island is not adequate for the average reader, who finds himself in the midst of his fellows and caught up in the sweep of historical events. To grasp the main thrust of the Bible, such a reader needs to discover in it an overall pattern that takes community and history seriously. The Bible indeed reveals the voice of the Alone speaking to the solitary soul, but even more it reveals the Alone as active in history, so that the great and small events of ordinary life signal his presence and will. As we have seen in so many other connections, there is no corner of life labeled "sacred," with the rest of life being relegated to "secular" status.

If the Hebrews took history seriously it was in large part because they took God's act of creation seriously. A solid world was brought into existence and what happened in it still bore the trademark of the one who invented it. God was to be recognized as much in daily life and in great public events—the rise of nations, wars, philosophic and religious movements—as in the messages received quietly by the individual in his privacy.

There are two basic ways of viewing the events of history. To the Hindu or Greek, they were part of a vast cycle, slowly and steadily repeating time after time. History was not going toward any final destination; it was simply manifesting at each stage what had already been and would be again when the time came. Traces of this viewpoint infiltrated Ecclesiastes, but are not typical of the Bible as a whole.

The cyclical view of time is still very much alive. For example, the modern theory of the expanding and contracting universe is a variant of this cosmology. It postulates a big bang, the long expansion of the universe, its eventual contraction, another big bang, another universe sent forth into space, and so on, possibly forever.

In the context of their times, the uniqueness of the ancient Hebrews was that they believed history has a destination. It is going someplace. And if we watch with discerning eyes, we have bountiful clues to pinpoint that direction. Our best chance for finding an overall pattern to the Bible is, therefore, to take history seriously, and to see God at work within it—beginning with the creation of the universe and coming down to headlines in today's newspaper.

This line of thought is nothing original. Many scholars, as well as ordinary readers, have discovered that the most fruitful approach is to see the Bible primarily as a book in which a particular kind of understanding is brought to bear upon the events of history. It is a drama. God is the central character.

That means that history is more than one random event after another. The Bible is concerned with what has been, is going on now, and what will be—all viewed in the light of the ultimate author of history. To put it another way, when we look at the slow unrolling of history, we discern it as the carrier of the X-Dimension. Through history there is mediated to us the smell of the locust trees and the sound of Vivaldi across the waters.

I propose to spend the rest of this book discussing the Bible as a five-act play. The author of the play, as I have indicated, is Yahweh himself. He built the stage when he created the universe, he wrote the basic script, he steps onto the stage as the principal actor when he is least expected. Even when he is not one of the visible actors, he is in the wings holding a prompter's book.

And yet, the way I have just put it is misleading. I made it sound as though our own actions on the stage of history were completely controlled, like the gyrations of puppets. And puppets are precisely what the Bible insists we are not. The reality is more like *commedia dell'arte*. We are told what the general plot is supposed to be, and are invited to improvise our roles as the play is presented on the stage. We are free, in fact, to create new roles never contemplated by the playwright, or to turn some of his characterizations upside down. We are the assistant playwrights, with the terrifying capacity to veto the best lines in the author's script. Still, he is not at our mercy either. He takes our revisions and improvisations and weaves them into the total plot, so that the ongoing play remains faithful to his vision. It is as though a child struck whatever keys on a piano took his fancy, and a great composer simultaneously struck other keys, thus creating a melody and harmony from their combined efforts.

If the Bible is a play, we can without distortion divide it into five acts, the traditional structure in the time of Shakespeare. The plot would be somewhat as follows:

ACT ONE: Creation and fall (myth and prehistory).

ACT TWO: Remedial measures (with special emphasis on the "Chosen People").

ACT THREE: The coming of the Messiah (how he fulfills old dreams and hopes).

ACT FOUR: The world we live in and its events (especially the role of Christianity and the Church).

ACT FIVE: The ultimate culmination (the "New Jerusalem").

What I shall do is pick out certain books or passages from the Bible and discuss them, in the framework of the five-act play. I hope to choose them in such a way that, taken together, they will constitute a mini-Bible as faithful as possible to the themes and proportions of the entire Bible.

This approach will inevitably do less than full justice to parts of the Bible, like Ecclesiastes and Job, which actually challenge certain of the dominant assumptions of the Bible. But I shall try to keep these recalcitrant books in mind, and show how they prove that the Bible, in the midst of recounting the meaning of history, carries on an internal dialogue with itself. In this private debate, multiple options of understanding are left open for the reader, even as he simultaneously finds himself pondering his lines in the Great Drama.

⋙ 17 ⋘

Creation
(Act One)

Everyone is familiar with this common movie technique: First you see a vast landscape, and then very gradually the focus shifts to a smaller and smaller scene and finally the screen is occupied by one face. Such is the pattern of the Bible. In the beginning the view on the screen is as vast as the universe itself. The focus narrows to mankind as a whole, then to the Hebrew people, and finally it narrows until one face, that of the strange rabbi, Jesus, fills the screen.

Chapters 1 and 2 of Genesis tell the story of a universe being willed into existence. Though it is a distortion to take this symbolic narrative and twist it to fit current theories of cosmology, it is interesting to note that there is a kind of logical progression in the stages of creation. God first creates light (the source of the energy by which we live) and moves by stages to simpler forms of life and then to the more complex:

Light
Separation of dry land from water
Vegetation
Heavenly bodies
Animals, birds, fish
Humanity

A squirrel or chimpanzee might feel there is human ethnocentricity in the order of events—and it is certainly true that the Bible everywhere makes a firm distinction between humanity with its special relation to the Creator, and the other forms of life. The climax of the whole process of creation comes on the sixth day when God brings mankind into existence.

There are actually two accounts of the creation of man. The more sophisticated one occurs in chapter 1, where man is created in the "image" of God, and given dominion over the other forms of life. In chapter 2, God forms him from the "dust of the ground" and breathes life into his nostrils. This second account is less evocative than the first: it is more like a magician's supreme achievement and implies little about the inner relation of man to his Creator.

The tale of man's creation, whether in its sophisticated or primitive version, should not be subjected too hastily to a theological analysis. The imagination ought first to be turned loose to visualize the stages poetically described in Genesis. And what a magnificent panorama it is! At the beginning, complete void or chaos. (It is unlikely that the ancient Hebrews made a sharp distinction between these two concepts.) There is the potentiality of a world, waiting to be called into existence by the Creator. Suddenly, the phenomenon of light, driving away the primal darkness. Then the separation of dry land from water. Then the bursting forth of life, as plants and trees march across the land, lighted by the sun* and the moon. With the creation of vegetation, there is now food for the animals, birds, and fish, which multiply everywhere. The great chain of being is working upward and the climax approaches as God creates his supreme work of art (1:26–31**):

> And God said, Let us make man in our image, after our likeness: and let them have dominion over the fish of the sea, and over the fowl of the air, and over the cattle, and over all the earth, and over every creeping thing that creepeth upon the earth. So God created man in his own image, in the image of God created he him; male and female created he them. And God blessed them, and God said unto them, Be fruitful, and multiply, and replenish the earth, and subdue it: and have dominion over the fish of the sea, and over the fowl of the air, and over every living thing that moveth upon the earth. . . . And God saw everything that he had made, and, behold, it was very good.

The word "dominion" is jolting to the modern ecological consciousness. And no recourse to dictionaries will tone it down. It sounds like an invitation to exterminate rare species if they get in the way of "progress," and to strip-mine the Appalachians until they lie flat.

Two considerations help to make the command more tolerable. First, the world to which the Bible addresses itself did not possess the chainsaw and heavy earth-moving equipment. A primitive technology set some limits on how savagely the earth could be exploited. More importantly, the Bible everywhere assumes that man does not really *own* the world over which he exercises dominion. Its ultimate owner is the One who brought it into existence. Man is merely a steward or caretaker, appoint-

---

*Logic breaks down here: the sun should be bracketed with light.

**Biblical quotations in this chapter are from the King James Version.

ed to manage daily affairs, but not authorized to destroy the very estate that has been entrusted to his care. All this means that man should exercise his dominion with becoming modesty, learning the rules by which nature lives and cooperating with nature. Viewed in this way, the modern ecological movement is thoroughly biblical in its ethic. The man who recklessly strips a whole landscape for transient coal is an irresponsible caretaker. The other man who learns to fight pests by the use of their natural biological enemies is operating within the limits set by nature, and preserving the Creator's good earth for use in subsequent generations.

The most mysterious assertion in the chapter 1 account of man's creation is that he was made in the "image of God." Only the most primitive religious thinking would insist that God is a physical being and we are small-scale replicas. The image of God does not mean that he has arms and legs and therefore we have them too. The phrase is saying something about the *relation* between the Creator and man.

At the very least, the "image of God" must mean that on our deepest level there is some kind of spiritual kinship between us and the One who created us. The question can be sharpened by asking what are the most basic differences between a human being and one of the more intelligent apes, such as a chimpanzee. One striking difference is that we can communicate with each other, even about things we cannot see, such as "justice." A second difference is that human beings have the freedom to know what is right but then go and do the exact opposite. Virtue is not programmed into us. As a result, it means something when we face a situation and make the right decision. The words "right" and "wrong" may not apply to animals at all, for their mode of behavior is given to them with their birth. A human being has the high glory of being able to choose: he can love his neighbor or hit him on the head with a blunt object. The "image of God" thus spells freedom and responsibility.

I suspect the mysterious phrase spells more. It is set in the context of the story of Creation, and in that story God himself is viewed first and foremost as one who summons something out of nothing or order out of chaos. Would it be stretching things too far to see in the image of God the capacity for creativity? Are we God's junior partners in creativity? And is that one of the major distinctions between us and all the other creatures that inhabit this globe? We love new things, and labor to create them. The animals are strict conservatives, clinging to their programmed habits. A beaver building a home for his family feels no need for new architectural styles. Eons ago some archetypal beaver solved all the problems of construction; the model that was good enough for great-grandfather beaver is good enough for his descendants. What beaver has ever shown the innovative spirit of a Frank Lloyd Wright? In the same way, the arts of painting and sculpture are human monopolies, if one disregards the occasional ape trained to wield brush and pigment. We seem to be God's junior partners in the creation of new things. God can create something from nothing; man can create something from anything. Art, cooking, gardening, the majestic work of the scientists—in all these the image of God is at work, inspiring in humanity the restless urge to make all things new.

So much for possible implications of the image of God. Meanwhile, we are in danger of losing sight of Adam as he explores his garden. But he does not need us. Eden is filled with "every tree that is pleasant to the sight, and good for food" (Genesis 2:9). The first man is left there in perfect freedom to do as he wishes, except for one prohibition: "Of the tree of the knowledge of good and evil, thou shalt not eat of it: for in the day that thou eatest thereof thou shalt surely die" (Genesis 2:17).

We must think of Adam as living in a world of indescribable beauty, with a boundless supply of all foods. It is a world in which conflict and exploitation do not exist. To live and breathe and move in such a world would have been a kind of continuous sacrament. Each fruit from a tree (with one exception), each fragrance from a flower would be the revelation of the Creator. The very act of being alive would be a hymn of praise.

Such is the vision. And it is not a vision restricted to the ancient Hebrews. The dream of a perfect world is practically worldwide. Often it is located in the far past or the infinite future; or it is on some other planet. Utopian dreamers have explored the haunting vision. So have grim-lipped political philosophers like Karl Marx, who denounced utopian thought as escapist while he created in his classless society a vision of a new Eden.

In all these intuitions of Eden, the underlying conviction is that the world as we see it—with droughts and floods, wars, muggings, and murders—is not the original or ultimate setting of the cosmic drama in which we speak our lines. We are exiles—from somewhere.

In his paradise, Adam need only obey the one prohibition placed upon his freedom. He is caretaker for Eden, and as such is granted the high honor of giving names to the animals as they are brought to him species by species. It is a peaceable kingdom, with newly made man exercising his benign dominion over nature by naming it.

But Adam lacks one thing. A companion. In the second creation story, God anesthetizes Adam and during his sleep removes a rib, which he then makes into a woman. In words that would be later be used to explain the binding nature of marriage, Adam welcomes his fellow citizen of Paradise (Genesis 2:23–24): "This is now bone of my bones, and flesh of my flesh: she shall be called Woman, because she was taken out of Man. Therefore shall a man leave his father and mother, and shall cleave unto his wife: and they shall be one flesh."

Thus, as we continue with Act One, we find Adam and Eve, in their naked innocence, inhabiting a world of perfect harmony and poignant beauty, free to love each other, free to love the animals, birds, and fishes, free most of all to love and praise the One who brought them into being and cares for all their needs. What more can they ask of life?

❧ 18 ❧

Fall

(Act One, continued)

The stage darkens. We are moving closer to the world we know from TV, newspapers, and personal observation. The characters in the human story, now two, begin to display psychological traits that we recognize inside ourselves. Though they live in a perfect garden, they are restless. The mere fact that the tree of good and evil is forbidden gives it a particular lure. What's so special about that tree? Why is God so touchy about it? What would happen if one took just one little bite? This must have seemed an innocent kind of fantasizing, like a husband who dreams of taking his secretary to Bermuda but returns each night to his wife.

Perhaps all this sounds as though I am reading motives into Adam and Eve. On the other hand, when these citizens of a perfect world find themselves confronted by the serpent, the woman puts up only the most nominal resistance, and the man none at all. They act as though they had already been infiltrated by rebellious thoughts.

It is interesting that the creature which finally brings their thoughts to a conscious level is a snake. Why? Perhaps to suggest the utterly alien. One can fraternize easily with animals and birds, but the sight of a snake, however harmless, is enough to provoke screams or brutal blows with a club. It is so . . . well, *different*.

The serpent in Eden takes the gradual approach. Translated into modern language, the dialogue goes like this:

SERPENT: Has God really told you not to eat from some of these trees?
EVE: He told us to leave the one in the middle alone. He won't even let us touch it.
SERPENT: What's wrong with touching it? Is it poisonous?

EVE: I don't know. But he says we'll die.

SERPENT: You don't believe that, do you?

EVE: Then why does God want us to leave that tree alone?

SERPENT: Aha, I'll tell you. I'll tell you something you don't know.

EVE: What's that?

SERPENT: He wants to keep you a child. He knows that once you taste a bit of that fruit, you will be like gods—

EVE: Like gods!

SERPENT: What's a god? Isn't it someone who knows the difference between good and evil?

EVE: What's good and evil?

SERPENT: Just take a bite and you'll find out. Then you'll be like gods. That's what he's holding back from you.

EVE: But he *said* we would die.

SERPENT: You'll be like gods, and gods don't die.

Eve's mind is racing ahead. What is really so wrong about sampling the tree? After all, God has encouraged them to enjoy the material abundance of their private garden. If the tree really is one to make you wise, what harm is there in that? Does God want her to be an ignorant little girl forever? It is exciting to be a human being, she discovers. All kinds of doors to experience are waiting to be opened.

But what about God's express command? Had they really understood him correctly? Perhaps at this point Eve's rising excitement blots out the memory of the stern and explicit command. At one time she knew it was a simple test of her obedience; now that knowledge is engulfed by a flood of emotions and desires.

Well, she tells herself, she will only do it once. Surely, if there are any penalties, they won't amount to much for a first offense, and if it seems wise—she begins to love this word—she can reform and be a good girl ever afterward.

So she eats the fruit.

Why Eve? Why not Adam?

We sense the possibility of male chauvinism. Most books, including the Bible, have been written by men, and men have never quite come to terms with the mysterious other sex. They pursue it and exploit it while at the same time demanding unearthly levels of purity and devotion. Perhaps some of Adam's earliest thoughts centered around the adorable, mysterious, and threatening otherness of his mate. And the long-forgotten writer and editor who put this story into its present form shared these thoughts. It seemed natural that the half-alien creature should be the one to test the limits of freedom.

To be fair to the ancient author, he does at least depict Eve as hesitating. When she offers to share the fruit with Adam, he does not hesitate. She has taken the responsibility; he is merely an innocent bystander. He is like a man lusting for a $20,000 gas guzzler, but waiting about signing the papers until his wife urges him to go ahead.

Quickly they learn fear—and shame. Once their relation with their creator was an easy companionship, but now God is to be avoided. One evening they take a stroll and hide among the trees when God approaches. "Where art thou?"* a voice calls. Adam stumbles through an explanation, "I heard thy voice in the garden, and I was afraid, because I was naked; and I hid myself."

God demands, "Who told thee that thou wast naked? Hast thou eaten of the tree, whereof I commanded thee that thou shouldest not eat?" Before their fall from innocence Adam and Eve had been no more aware of their nudity than an animal of its fur. All that is changed.

The Bible now rises to one of its peaks of human understanding. Forgetting that he was ready enough to follow the bad example of his wife, Adam puts the blame on her: "The woman whom thou gavest to be with me, she gave me of the tree, and I did eat." Eve also tries to slip out from under any responsibility: "The serpent beguiled me, and I did eat." The poor serpent is left bearing the whole burden of guilt. But at least Eve uses a snake as her scapegoat, whereas Adam uses his wife.

Apparently, the serpent was originally some kind of creature that walked on its feet. But when God begins to deal out penalties, the serpent is transformed into the familiar snake, crawling on its belly, and locked in murderous conflict with

---

*Biblical quotations in this chapter are from the King James Version, Genesis 3.

humanity. The woman is condemned to painful childbearing, and subjected to the rule of her husband. Adam is sentenced to a lifetime of hard labor: ". . . Cursed is the ground for thy sake: in sorrow shalt thou eat of it all the days of thy life; Thorns also and thistles shall it bring forth to thee; and thou shalt eat the herb of the field; In the sweat of thy face shalt thou eat bread, till thou return unto the ground; for out of it wast thou taken: for dust thou art, and unto dust shalt thou return."

God clothes the pair in skins—sad badges of lost innocence—and drives them out of Eden. As they begin their trek through the thistles of the everyday earth we can imagine them looking back at Paradise, perhaps half-planning some stratagem to regain it. But it is guarded by cherubim and a flaming sword.

By this point in Genesis the movement out of the mists of myth and legend and into the plain light of historical day is close at hand. Disobedience is abroad; the perfection of Eden is corrupted; the destiny of death awaits all human beings. And, one imagines, Adam and Eve have advanced faster in psychological age than in physical. They are no longer innocent young creatures, almost like lovable animals. There are wrinkles in their brows, and a hunted and hunting look in their eyes. Their glances hide as much as they reveal. They have entered the circle of the fully human and therefore half-miserable. They will daydream of returning to their innocent home and will sometimes seem to get close to it, but never quite reenter its gate. They carry with them everywhere the divided consciousness of creatures who bear the mark of their creator but also the mark of their alienation from him.

It might be argued, without contradiction, that Adam and Eve both fell and rose. They fell into disobedience and lost their easy familiarity with God. If that was ever to be recovered, it would have to be through the initiative of God, not their own. But at the same time, they fell upward. The snake was not lying when he promised them new knowledge if they would only taste of good and evil and know, with their very tastebuds, the difference. They are now adults. What might have been at most a hazy, theoretical awareness of a possible not-good (unsubstantial as the darkness that exists only because we first know light) has been exchanged for existential knowledge. Across the abyss of time, we stretch hands to our first ancestors and welcome them into the world in which we were born.

The tale of Adam and Eve is one of the points where Jewish and Christian interpretations diverge. Jewish thought has concentrated on the personal sin of the primal pair, whereas Christian theology—especially under the influence of Paul—has developed the doctrine of original sin. Viewed this way, the fall of Adam and Eve becomes a collective thing. It is as though all humanity is like one tree with many leaves. If a blight penetrates any part of the tree, it swiftly spreads to every branch and leaf. Or to use a modern metaphor, it is as though sin entered our genes in the Garden of Eden, and remains part of our genetic structure. Theologians differ on how complete the corruption is, but the central Christian tradition holds that God himself must shoulder the burden of restoration to innocence and wholeness.

Where are we at the moment? Approaching the end of Act One of the divine drama. We have been told that the central actor is God. It is he who by an act of his will turns nothing into something, a universe. He creates that special form of life we call man and endows him with his very own "image." He sets the human adventure in the midst of a beautiful garden and turns his creatures free except for one small tabu—the prohibition against eating from a certain tree. To make Adam's happiness complete, he creates a wife for him. To the two of them and their descendants he gives "dominion" over the lesser forms of life. Paradise doesn't last. Adam and Eve eat the forbidden fruit and are expelled from their garden.

❧ 19 ❧

From Myth Toward History
(Act One, concluded)

In chapter 4 of Genesis we see normal human life beginning. For one thing, Eve becomes pregnant. She gives birth to Abel, a shepherd, and to Cain, a farmer. In the subsequent history of these two sons one senses perhaps the lingering conviction that the life of a herdsman is better, somehow more innocent, than that of a farmer. The movement toward agriculture was not yet universal; many inhabitants of the Middle East, like the Bedouins today, scorned the farmer and his daily drudgery on one patch of soil.

This may help to explain why we see God pleased with Abel's offering and critical of Cain's. Poor Cain's face drops, and God says to him,* "Why art thou wroth? and why is thy countenance fallen? If thou doest well, shalt thou not be accepted? and if thou doest not well, sin lieth at the door." Cain still does not know what he has done wrong.

It requires little imagination to feel considerable sympathy for Cain. We can imagine him brooding over the injustice of life. His feelings rise to a fury of madness when his brother, Abel, chats with him. Here is the pampered darling basking in God's favor; and here is Cain, working long hours in soil choked with weeds and thistles, and getting nothing but blame. Perhaps Cain is one of those inarticulate people whose feelings remain bottled up until they explode with murderous violence. Murderous is the right word. Cain murders Abel.

There is now a parallel to what happened after Adam and Eve ate the fatal fruit. God knows something has gone wrong. "Where's your brother?" he demands. A tone of insolence comes into human speech when Cain replies: "Why are you

---

* Biblical quotations in this chapter are from the King James Version.

asking me? Am I being paid to look after that brother of mine?"

God brushes aside that question, to be heard from so many human lips in subsequent millennia. "Do you know what you've done? The voice of your brother's very blood is calling out to me from the soil you are working."

And now we must abandon colloquial English and permit God the stately language of the King James Version as he pronounces judgment on the world's first murderer. The penalty is exile: "And now art thou cursed from the earth, which hath opened her mouth to receive thy brother's blood from thy hand; When thou tillest the ground, it shall not henceforth yield unto thee her strength; a fugitive and a vagabond shalt thou be in the earth." God does permit himself one act of mercy. He puts a mark on Cain as a warning that no one is to kill him.

It is interesting that the first murder was fratricide. The author of Genesis evidently wanted to present murder at its almost-worst; only patricide or matricide would have evoked a deeper sense of horror.

Life goes on, even for the murderer. Later we find him establishing himself east of Eden and becoming the father of a son, Enoch. He then founds a city which he names for his son. And though the mark God has put upon him is his shame, it is also his protection.

From the viewpoint of Genesis, there is a neat and inevitable progression from the eating of forbidden fruit to the first murder. At one time humanity, in the persons of Adam and Eve, had been centered in God, and it was therefore easy and natural to obey his laws. But once the relation with God was distorted, every other relation was out of joint. All latent impulses for evil were set free. Soon murder and every other crime flourished.

As God looks down upon the earth, observing its welter of violence, he is tempted to cancel the whole human experiment. But he does see one man with whom he can be pleased. This is Noah. God decides to spare him and his family, and thus allow humanity a fresh start. The story is told in chapters 6 through 8.

First, God commands Noah to make a large boat. When the great flood comes, the ark will house Noah and his family and all species of animals. They can float out the flood and reestablish life on the earth when the deluge comes to an end. The choice of a worldwide flood as a way of cleansing the earth from universal sin was natural enough, since the Middle East, with its great rivers and flash floods, had often been inundated.

The ark is lifted by rising waters; soon even the mountains are covered. The whole future of life on the earth is huddled in Noah's floating zoo. For a hundred and fifty days the flood lasts. Finally, God calls it off. Noah dispatches a dove which returns with an olive leaf. The earth is re-emerging. God tells him and all the other inhabitants of the ark to venture forth on dry land.

God then seems to have second thoughts about his almost complete extermination of life. Perhaps he sadly recognizes that he has demanded more of the human race than it can deliver; he must reconcile himself to a slow process of rehabilitation. In this more compassionate frame of mind, he promises, "I will not again curse the ground any more for man's sake; for the imagination of man's heart is evil from his youth; neither will I again smite any more every thing living, as I have done."

At this point, we have the second biblical covenant. The first was the implied covenant between God and the two inhabitants of Eden. The second is similar in that is applies to the whole human race rather than specifically to the Hebrews. In chapter 9 the details of the covenant are spelled out. God blesses Noah and his family and commands them to multiply and fill the almost empty earth. Their stewardship over lesser creatures is reemphasized, and they are left free to eat anything they wish except "flesh with the life thereof, which is the blood thereof." God for his part promises no more universal floods. So that he will not forget, he establishes a symbol for this covenant—a rainbow—and promises that when he sees it he will be reminded of his promise.

Noah emerges as the hero of this just-in-time rescue of the human race. If he had not favorably impressed God, there would have been no ark and no humankind. At the same time, he is no paragon of virtue. When we next see him he is in a drunken stupor. If he was the best humanity had to offer, God's long-range plans to undo the catastrophe of Adam and Eve would be time-consuming indeed.

The mists of prehistory now begin to blow away, and actual history confronts us. By chapter 11, with its tale of the Tower of Babel, we have real history converted into a symbol of mankind's incurable desire to be master of its own fate, "to stand on its own two feet." There were real towers, built by the real Babylonians and Assyrians, to prove their greatness. As we noted earlier, the author/editor saw in such towers the evil fruits of man's desire to be independent of his maker; to be, in fact, like gods. In the same chapter, Abram (who later is renamed Abraham) steps upon the stage and ushers in the age of patriarchs. Mythology has served its purpose. Now is the time for history.

As one looks back at the first few chapters of Genesis, the wonder grows. The raw materials are not original. The Middle East was full of legends—creation myths, mysterious trees, floods. The achievement of the author/editor is the more amazing when one sees how he uses these folk tales to convey the most profound religious and psychological truths. Adam is Hebrew for man, and Eve is Hebrew for life or living. The traditional tales as reshaped in Genesis are the story of the Life of Everyman and Everywoman.

⁂ 20 ⁂

A Special People
(Act Two)

And so the curtain goes down on Act One. Act Two, the special history of the Chosen People, begins. Eden fades farther and farther into legends; historical names like Canaan and Egypt begin to appear.

The Middle East is in a time of great unrest. In the third millennium B.C. important civilizations had developed there. Then came the inroads of various Semitic peoples, pouring in from the desert and destroying the great cities. These migrations continued for centuries until the invaders in their turn created new civilizations. What are now Israel and Jordan were not spared. In the third millennium they had cities, fortifications, and temples, all of which sank into ruins.

The biblical story now centers around the patriarch, Abram (which means exalted father; his later name, Abraham, means father of a multitude). The universal restlessness is in his heart. We see him and his extended family leaving the ancient city of Ur and slowly progressing toward Canaan. Before reaching their destination, they come to Haran and settle there. Abraham then has a crucial experience of the divine presence, which ever afterward was to shape the Hebrew understanding of their destiny (Genesis 12:1–3*):

> Now the LORD said to Abram, "Go from your country and your kindred and your father's house to the land that I will show you. And I will make of you a great nation, and I will bless you, and make your name great, so that you will be a blessing. I will bless those who bless you, and him who curses you I will curse; and by you all the families of the earth will bless themselves."

---

* Biblical quotations in this chapter are from the Revised Standard Version.

Abraham asks no questions. He takes his family and followers and resumes the journey to Canaan. In the course of these wanderings he has other encounters with God. On one of these occasions the Lord commands him to look at the sky (Genesis 15:1–6) and try to count the stars; his descendants will be equally numerous. Then comes the quiet, almost parenthetical statement: "And he [Abraham] believed the LORD; and he [God] reckoned it to him as righteousness." This is a theme later to receive much fuller treatment in the New Testament, as a foundation for the doctrine of justification by faith.

At one encounter the promises of God are made into a formal covenant. All the Land of Canaan will be the homeland of Abraham's descendants. The token of the covenant is circumcision (Genesis 17:9–14):

> And God said to Abraham, "As for you, you shall keep my covenant, you and your descendants after you throughout their generations. This is my covenant, which you shall keep, between me and you and your descendants after you: Every male among you shall be circumcised. You shall be circumcised in the flesh of your foreskins, and it shall be a sign of the covenant between me and you. He that is eight days old among you shall be circumcised; every male throughout your generations, whether born in your house, or bought with your money from any foreigner who is not of your offspring, both he that is born in your house and he that is bought with your money, shall be circumcised. So shall my covenant be in your flesh an everlasting covenant. Any uncircumcised male who is not circumcised in the flesh of his foreskin shall be cut off from his people; he has broken my covenant."

Another time, Abraham's faith is stretched to the breaking point. In Genesis 17:15–21, God promises that he shall have a son. Abraham (aged a hundred) and Sarah (aged ninety) can only laugh at the absurd idea. But the son, Isaac, is born in due course.

Abraham's faith receives its cruelest test when in chapter 22 God commands him to offer up Isaac, the blessing of his old age, as a human sacrifice. The story is one of the many short masterpieces of narration that one finds in the Old Testament. We see the aged father cutting firewood in preparation for the offering. We trace his progress during a three-day journey to the place of sacrifice. We hear his ambiguous words to the two young men accompanying him, as he tells them he must go apart to worship. Next—with what irony!—he hands the wood to Isaac and tells him to carry it. They come to the place that God has designated, and the curiously passive Isaac lets his father bind him and stretch him out on the firewood. Abraham grasps his knife and moves to plunge it in. At the very last moment, an angelic voice commands him to stop—" 'Now I know that you fear God, seeing you have not withheld your son, your only son, from me.' " Freed from his hideous duty, Abraham looks up and sees a ram caught in a thicket by his horns. So a burnt offering is made after all.

It is impossible to read the story without a tug at the throat and dark questions about the goodness of God. Some see in the tale simply the reflection of a time when human sacrifice was gradually being replaced by animal offerings. Others find it too similar to contemporary religious fanatics who believe they have heard God ordering murder and arson and have hastened to obey. Perhaps it is best viewed simply as the final test of Abraham's trust in God.

We come now to a series of stories about Abraham's descendants, such as the charming tale of how Isaac wooed Rebekah for his wife (chapter 24). Meanwhile, at the age of one hundred seventy-five, Abraham quietly passes away. He stands out in retrospect as a morally impressive figure, fair in his dealings with others, striving always to do the will of God though his faith is sometimes sorely tested. The same cannot be said of all his descendants. The rivalry of Isaac's twin sons, Jacob and Esau, is almost like a picaresque novel in which crafty Jacob constantly tricks his slower-witted brother. In one episode (Genesis 25:29–34) hairy Esau is famished from work in the scorching fields and sees his brother stirring a mess of pottage. Jacob agrees to provide a helping in return for Esau's birthright. Another time Jacob, following the advice of his mother, Rebekah, disguises himself in Esau's clothes and a hairy goatskin, thus tricking the nearly blind Isaac into blessing the wrong brother. These unedifying tales may not have much clear religious significance, but they illustrate once again that the biblical portrait artists retained all the warts on the noble patriarchal faces.

Yet there is more to Jacob than the trickster. In chapter 28 he dreams of seeing a ladder reaching from earth to heaven; on it angels ascend and descend. Above it stands the Lord himself, who speaks to Jacob and makes the same promises he had made to Abraham. This is an example of how the God revealed in the Bible can take rather unpromising persons and reshape their lives. From now on Jacob is at the command of God.

Beginning with chapter 37 and continuing to the end of Genesis, we have the beautifully wrought story of Joseph, eleventh son of Jacob. Joseph's personality comes through sharply. He is quick-witted and capable, with a genius both for getting into difficulties and adroitly getting out of them.

It is sometimes difficult to tell whether Joseph has the naiveté of innocence or is subtly asserting himself. As a boy he knew that he was his father's favorite, and this circumstance might have dictated a certain tact with his brothers. Instead, we find him recounting dreams such as the one in which the sheaves of his brothers all bow to his own sheaf. The brothers finally have more than they are willing to take. They first conspire to murder him, then—horrified a little by thoughts of fratricide—they decide to sell him into slavery and pretend to their father that a wild beast has devoured him.

A caravan bound for Egypt conveniently comes by, and soon Joseph is on his way to the land where he will be a slave. His master, Potiphar, soon recognizes that this is no common slave. He puts him in charge of all his possessions and affairs. But now Joseph faces another crisis: Potiphar's wife. Without circumlocutions, she commands him, "Lie with me." Joseph pleads to be let off. This is no way to repay the kindness and trust of his master. This answer does not satisfy single-minded Mrs. Potiphar. One day she catches him alone in the house and renews her demand. She seizes his garment in her hand; he breaks away and flees, presumably stark naked. The scorned woman tells her husband that this Hebrew has tried to seduce her. Potiphar is furious and orders Joseph confined in prison.

But even here his superior abilities do not fail him. Soon Potiphar appoints him to administer the prison.

In jail, Joseph establishes a reputation as an interpreter of dreams. This brings him into contact with Pharaoh. The king has disturbing dreams of fat cattle and lean, plump ears of grain and diseased ears. He sends for Joseph, who promptly interprets the dream—seven years of good crops, seven years of famine. Not content with explaining the dreams, Joseph goes on to give some practical advice (Genesis 41:33–36):

> "Now therefore let Pharaoh select a man discreet and wise, and set him over the land of Egypt. Let Pharaoh proceed to appoint overseers over the land, and take the fifth part of the produce of the land of Egypt during the seven plenteous years. And let them gather all the food of these good years that are coming, and lay up grain under the authority of Pharaoh for food in the cities, and let them keep it. That food shall be a reserve for the land against the seven years of famine which are to befall the land of Egypt, so that the land may not perish through the famine."

Pharaoh looks around for such a person and soon decides that Joseph is the best qualified. He designates him as viceroy of Egypt, and entrusts to him all the preparations for the time of famine. As we have grown to expect, Joseph is a glittering success in this task, the savior of Egypt.

It is at this point that the annals of Joseph come full circle. Famine is ravaging Canaan, and Jacob sends ten of his sons to buy grain from the Egyptians. There follows the scene in which Joseph recognizes his brothers, who had sold him into bondage. But they do not recognize him in the imposing court official who stands before them. The story moves to the climax when Joseph reveals his identity (45:4–9):

> So Joseph said to his brothers, "Come near to me, I pray you." And they came near. And he said, "I am your brother, Joseph, whom you sold into Egypt. And now do not be distressed, or angry with yourselves, because you sold me here; for God sent me before you to preserve life. For the famine has been in the land these two years; and there are yet five years in which there will be neither plowing nor harvest. And God sent me before you to preserve for you a remnant on earth, and to keep alive for you many survivors.

So it was not you who sent me here, but God; and he has made me a father to Pharaoh, and lord of all his house and ruler over all the land of Egypt. Make haste and go up to my father and say to him, 'Thus says your son Joseph, God has made me lord of all Egypt; come down to me, do not tarry.' "

Jacob (whose other name is Israel) travels with the promise of the same God who guided Abraham ringing in his ears (Genesis 46:1-7):

So Israel took his journey with all that he had, and came to Beer-sheba, and offered sacrifices to the God of his father Isaac. And God spoke to Israel in visions of the night, and said, "Jacob, Jacob." And he said, "Here am I." Then he said, "I am God, the God of your father; do not be afraid to go down to Egypt; for I will there make of you a great nation. I will go down with you to Egypt, and I will also bring you up again; and Joseph's hand shall close your eyes." Then Jacob set out from Beer-sheba; and the sons of Israel carried Jacob their father, their little ones, and their wives, in the wagons which Pharaoh had sent to carry him. They also took their cattle and their goods, which they had gained in the land of Canaan, and came into Egypt, Jacob and all his offspring with him, his sons, and his sons' sons with him, his daughters, and his sons' daughters; all his offspring he brought with him into Egypt.

The story of Joseph illustrates one of the dominant themes of the Bible. God can bring good out of evil. Later we shall see him using the Pagan Assyrians to chastise the rebellious Hebrews. Here, in the tale of Joseph, we have what first seems yet another unedifying story—a lad sold into slavery by his jealous brothers. But good comes of it. If Joseph had not become viceroy of Egypt, he would not have been in a position to rescue his family during the great famine. Thus it was that the basest human motives contributed to the long-range plans of God for his Chosen People.

One might go further and argue that the prolonged residence of the Hebrews in Egypt, which began with a frightened boy being transferred to a caravan of slave traders, accomplished what centuries of wandering had not quite done. It made a nation of the Hebrews. When it came time for them to escape from Egypt, they knew who they were.

≫ 21 ≪

Let My People Go
(Act Two, continued)

As the end of Genesis approaches, we find the descendants of Jacob living in Egypt, protected by the favor of Pharaoh and his viceroy, Joseph. It seems that their wanderings have come to an end. For centuries, even millennia, they have been a semi-nomadic people, milling about in the great ethnic crazy quilt of the Middle East, seeking pasturelands and water. In this they were no different from most of their Semitic neighbors. In that ancient world, passports seem to have been unknown, and tribes could drift from one land to another.

How long the Hebrews dwelt in Egypt we do not know for sure. It was certainly long enough for memories to grow dim and for ways of life to change. The old stories of their Father Abraham undoubtedly circulated around evening fires and stirred twinges of nostalgia, but meanwhile here they were in Egypt, learning the ways of a more sophisticated civilization, and—at least at times—not making out too badly.

There is no reason to believe that every last Hebrew joined the migration into Egypt at the time of Joseph. Some probably continued their slow drift from one country to another. Others were already in Canaan and would in due time welcome their fellow Hebrews when the invasion of the Promised Land began.

The curtain goes up again and reveals the Hebrews still in Egypt. It is probably the thirteenth century B.C. We learn from the Book of Exodus that the Hebrew minority had grown large enough to be an anxiety to the Egyptian authorities. A Pharaoh who could never have known Joseph now sits on the throne. He is afraid that in time of war the Hebrews will fight on the enemy side and seize the opportunity to escape.

The natives of Egypt, egged on by Pharaoh, set about making the lives of the Hebrews as onerous as possible. They are conscripted to build cities under the menace of the foreman's lash; they are equally driven when they work in the fields. The old, easygoing days are over.

Pharaoh does not stop with the imposition of hard labor. He turns to genocide, commanding the Hebrew midwifes to kill all male babies. When he finds them neglecting these orders, they explain that the Hebrew women are so lively that they give birth before a midwife can arrive. Frustrated, Pharaoh issues new commands to the Egyptians—to throw all male Hebrew babies into the Nile.

Now comes the turning point with the birth of Moses. His mother leaves him in a basket by the edge of the river and hopes for the best. In an example of how gentiles may do the work of God without intending it, Pharaoh's daughter comes on the child and hires a Hebrew woman, who happens to be the baby's mother, to take care of him. When the child is old enough his mother turns him over to Pharaoh's daughter who adopts him as her son. Thus the future liberator of the Hebrews was as much at home in the Egyptian culture as in the Hebrew.

Moses could have cast his lot with the dominant Egyptians, but did not. One day, after he grows up, he sees an Egyptian beating a Hebrew. He coolly looks around to make sure there are no witnesses, then kills the Egyptian and buries him in the sand. Next day, when he tries to stop a fight between two Hebrews, one of them asks an alarming question (Exodus 2:14*): " 'Who made you a prince and a judge over us? Do you mean to kill me as you killed the Egyptian?' " Evidently, word of his deed of the day before is getting around. It finally reaches Pharaoh, who tries to kill Moses; the latter flees to Midian.

Here we encounter the archetypal pattern of withdrawal and return. We will see it constantly repeated in the life of Jesus when he alternated between periods of intense and public activity and times when he journeyed to wilderness or mountain. It is a common enough pattern in "real life," as when Charles DeGaulle withdrew to his country retreat and waited

---

* Biblical quotations in this chapter are from the Revised Standard Version.

passively until he was called back to rule France. It is a typical pattern for culture heroes. The hero returns with new strengths and insights from his time of withdrawal.

While living in Midian, Moses meets the priest, Jethro, and marries one of his daughters. Meanwhile, Pharaoh dies, but his successor is no improvement. The oppression of the Hebrews continues, until at last their outcries reach Yahweh himself, who remembers his promises to Abraham, Isaac, and Jacob. He chooses Moses for the task of liberation.

Why Moses? Not because he is an experienced general or charismatic political leader. One gets the impression that he is usually a rather cautious person—after all, he looked around in every direction before killing the Egyptian. He also has a speech impediment, so that his brother Aaron has to repeat his words. He has few obvious qualities of leadership.

And that is the point. God does not need a Churchill or Roosevelt, still less a Stalin, for this task. All he requires is someone who will unflinchingly obey orders. The ultimate general of his liberation operation is God himself.

The Bible is filled with accounts of people who are suddenly confronted by God and given assignments. He is always brisk and businesslike. He brushes aside protestations of inadequacy, as when Moses, confronted by God, urges him to select a better qualified person.

Moses is indeed taken by surprise. Who would expect an epiphany while tending a flock on Mount Sinai? But all at once, he sees a bush that burns and burns and is never consumed. It is a classical example of numinous experience, as a voice calls from inside the bush (Exodus 3:4–12):

> When the LORD saw that he turned aside to see, God called to him out of the bush, "Moses, Moses!" And he said, "Here am I." Then he said, "Do not come near; put off your shoes from your feet, for the place on which you are standing is holy ground." And he said, "I am the God of your father, the God of Abraham, the God of Isaac, and the God of Jacob." And Moses hid his face, for he was afraid to look at God.
>
> Then the LORD said, "I have seen the affliction of my people who are in Egypt, and have heard their cry because of their task-

masters; I know their sufferings, and I have come down to deliver them out of the hand of the Egyptians, and to bring them up out of that land to a good and broad land, a land flowing with milk and honey, to the place of the Canaanites, the Hittites, the Amorites, the Perizzites, the Hivites, and the Jebusites. And now, behold, the cry of the people of Israel has come to me, and I have seen the oppression with which the Egyptians oppress them. Come, I will send you to Pharaoh that you may bring forth my people, the sons of Israel, out of Egypt." But Moses said to God, "Who am I that I should go to Pharaoh, and bring the sons of Israel out of Egypt?" He said, "But I will be with you; and this shall be the sign for you, that I have sent you: when you have brought forth the people out of Egypt, you shall serve God upon this mountain."

One has the impression that Moses' mind is operating slowly but profoundly. He is worried that people may want to know the name of this God. In many ancient societies, a name is not just the functional equivalent of a computer number. It is the very power and essence of the person bearing the name. In the Bible, a name is often a descriptive statement. So it is with the divine name. God reveals it to Moses: I Am Who I Am. That is, God's reality does not depend on anyone or anything else. He is self-existent.

God, however, does not intend to get bogged down in questions and answers. He wants Moses to move ahead with the job at hand. He instructs him to bring the elders of Israel together and to assure them that God will lead them out of bondage into the land long ago promised to Abraham. Moses and Aaron assemble the people on Mount Sinai. Speaking through Aaron, Moses conveys the divine message. To establish his credentials, he demonstrates the magic rod God has given him which turns into a snake.

Moses and Aaron next appear before Pharaoh to plead the case for their people. The two Hebrews begin softly, but the absolute ruler confronting them belongs to the no-nonsense school of government. He is not going to let a couple of slaves tell *him* how to run *his* country (Exodus 5:1-7):

Afterward Moses and Aaron went to Pharaoh and said, "Thus says the LORD, the God of Israel, 'Let my people go, that they may hold a feast to me in the wilderness.' " But Pharaoh said, "Who is the LORD, that I should heed his voice and let Israel go? I do not know the LORD, and moreover I will not let Israel go." Then they said, "The God of the Hebrews has met with us; let us go, we pray, a three days' journey into the wilderness, and sacrifice to the LORD our God, lest he fall upon us with pestilence or with the sword." But the king of Egypt said to them, "Moses and Aaron, why do you take the people away from their work? Get to your burdens." And Pharaoh said, "Behold, the people of the land are now many and you make them rest from their burdens!" The same day Pharaoh commanded the taskmasters of the people and their foremen, "You shall no longer give the people straw to make bricks, as heretofore; let them go and gather straw for themselves."

The taskmasters and foremen eagerly enforce the new rules, and when the Hebrews send a delegation to Pharaoh they receive no sympathy. Pharaoh has a theory to explain why they are discontented (Exodus 5:17): " 'You are idle, you are idle; therefore you say, "Let us go and sacrifice to the LORD." ' " When Moses meets the Hebrew delegation they scold him for having antagonized Pharaoh and put their lives in jeopardy. This is an early instance of the kind of resistance he constantly encounters from his own people when they face difficult situations. A military analyst would not have given these fearful folk much chance.

There now ensues an epic competition between Moses and the Egyptian magicians. Moses turns his rod into a snake and performs a series of additional miracles, but the Egyptians each time match his feat. Several times Pharaoh promises to liberate the Hebrew people, but always changes his mind. God's patience now comes to an end. It is time for his ultimate power to be demonstrated. Death stalks the land and claims the firstborn of every Egyptian, even the son of Pharaoh. The Hebrews, who have smeared their door frames with the blood of a sacrificial lamb, escape unharmed.

Pharaoh at last admits defeat. He gives permission for the Hebrews to depart, and the Egyptian people insist that this be at once. Next comes the scene that has stirred the imagination of so many artists: the countless Hebrews leaving in such haste that there is no time to put leaven in their dough, the steady tramp of cattle, the woolly panorama of sheep and goats.

But never trust a Pharaoh. No sooner have the Hebrews left than he decides he has lost a good source of cheap labor. So, still convinced that swords and chariots are a ruler's final authority, he sets out in pursuit and encounters them by the sea.

We have to imagine the contrast. Pharaoh's army would have been superbly trained, hardened in war, equipped with the latest models of chariots. Opposed to it is a loosely organized horde of civilians, armed with primitive weapons, unskilled in war. No wonder they are quick to lose heart. As the greatest miracle in their national life is about to dazzle their eyes, they are busy worrying (Exodus 14:11-12): ". . . They said to Moses, 'Is it because there are no graves in Egypt that you have taken us away to die in the wilderness? What have you done to us, in bringing us out of Egypt? Is not this what we said to you in Egypt, "Let us alone and let us serve the Egyptians?" For it would have been better for us to serve the Egyptians than to die in the wilderness.' " And who can blame them? Humanly speaking, they face massacre—or, at best, a return to slavery.

God commands Moses to lift up his rod and divide the sea. Moses obeys. A strong east wind blows all night, dividing the waters. The Hebrews advance dry-shod. The Egyptians pursue them. The waters return. Not one Egyptian in their great army survives.

For a while at least the Hebrews will now believe that what Moses has been telling them is true. And one of them, moved to poetry, composes one of the oldest sections of the Bible, to celebrate this incredible victory. This poem is the closest thing we have to an eyewitness account (15:1-18). Here is how it begins:

"I will sing to the LORD, for he has triumphed gloriously;
    the horse and his rider he has thrown into the sea.
The LORD is my strength and my song,
    and he has become my salvation;
this is my God, and I will praise him,
    my father's God, and I will exalt him.

The LORD is a man of war;
  the LORD is his name.

"Pharaoh's chariots and his host he cast into the sea;
  and his picked officers are sunk in the Red Sea.
The floods cover them;
  they went down into the depths like a stone.
Thy right hand, O LORD, glorious in power,
  thy right hand, O LORD, shatters the enemy."

⁂ 22 ⁂

"I Am Who I Am" Speaks
(Act Two, continued)

The crossing of the Red Sea might seem the ultimate miracle in the annals of the Hebrew People. But it is merely preliminary to the revelation at Mount Sinai. Meanwhile, the throng wanders with their livestock in the wilderness, fighting and winning a battle with the Kingdom of Amalek, eating miraculous manna, and complaining about the scarcity of water.

Through Moses, God commands the people to consecrate themselves for the impending revelation (chapter 19). On the morning of the third day there is thunder and lightening, earthquakes, thick smoke, and the sound of trumpets. God is at the summit of the mountain while the people, warned by him, remain below. Only Moses and Aaron are summoned to the holy presence. God now proclaims the Ten Commandments (Exodus 20:1–17*):

---

* Biblical quotations in this chapter are from the Revised Standard Version.

And God spoke all these words, saying,

"I am the LORD your God, who brought you out of the land of Egypt, out of the house of bondage.

"You shall have no other gods before me.

"You shall not make yourself a graven image, or any likeness of anything that is in heaven above, or that is in the earth beneath, or that is in the water under the earth; you shall not bow down to them or serve them; for I the LORD your God am a jealous God, visiting the iniquity of the fathers upon the children to the third and the fourth generation of those who hate me, but showing steadfast love to thousands of those who love me and keep my commandments.

"You shall not take the name of the LORD your God in vain; for the LORD will not hold him guiltless who takes his name in vain.

"Remember the sabbath day, to keep it holy. Six days you shall labor, and do all your work; but the seventh day is a sabbath to the LORD your God; in it you shall not do any work, you, or your son, or your daughter, your manservant, or your maidservant, or your cattle, or the sojourner who is within your gates; for in six days the LORD made heaven and earth, the sea, and all that is in them, and rested the seventh day; therefore the LORD blessed the sabbath day and hallowed it.

"Honor your father and your mother, that your days may be long in the land which the LORD your God gives you.

"You shall not kill.

"You shall not commit adultery.

"You shall not steal.

"You shall not bear false witness against your neighbor.

"You shall not covet your neighbor's house; you shall not covet your neighbor's wife, or his manservant, or his maidservant, or his ox, or his ass, or anything that is your neighbor's."

Some of these commandments sound like the much later Book of Proverbs. They are the basic minimum needed to hold a society together. But these "secular" commandments are set in a theocratic framework. God first of all commands primacy among the gods. He does not explicitly say there are no other gods—but he must come first. It may well be, as some have speculated, that originally the Hebrews worshiped a God thought to be especially associated with Mount Sinai, as other nations had geographically-based divinities. With time, geographic limits faded away, and only the God was left. For all practical purposes, God proclaims himself as such on Mount Sinai.

God puts "religion" first. The firm foundation on which everyday morality must rest is the omnipresent fact of God. This is emphasized further in the commandment against graven images. One might ask—what's wrong about making a statue of a crocodile or human being? The facts of religious history are that the ancient Middle East was literally idolatrous. Statues were in temples everywhere, and sacrifices, sometimes of human beings, were offered to them. Often associated with idolatry was sacred prostitution. But the fundamental flaw with idolatry was that it was a creation of human fantasy.

God threatens to punish even the third and fourth generation of those who bow down to idols. At first glance, this seems blatantly unfair. Why should a child be punished because his great-grandfather sacrificed to an idol? From our individualistic way of viewing responsibility, the dilemma cannot be resolved. But the Old Testament, though it has a keen sensitivity to the rights and dignity of the individual, is centered still more in the organic groupings of humanity: family, clan, nation, humankind as a whole. If a blight strikes one limb of a tree it will spread to the other limbs. In our times, for example, the consequences of the extravagant use of gasoline by parents and grandparents are daily visited on the young man or woman who has just secured a driving license.

Having established the fundamental basis for his commands—that God comes first—the voice at Sinai proceeds to spell out some of the implications. For instance, 20:7: "'You shall not take the name of the LORD your God in vain.'" This commandment forbids more than casual "cussing." We have seen that to the ancient Hebrews a person's name is bound up with his very essence. In the Old Testament there is a profound reverence enveloping the ultimate name of God. All sorts of substitutes are used in place of the holy name.

Where does this leave us with the prohibition against taking God's name "in vain"? It means that the holy name is to be used with caution and reverence. To employ the name, say, in an oath that is then lightly disregarded is to use it in vain, frivolously.

Next comes the commandment for the observance of the weekly Sabbath. This represents a point where religious convictions and social needs come together. The idea of a periodic day of rest and renewal does not require a divine revelation. The atheistic Soviets observe Sunday without giving God the credit. But the biblical command to honor the Sabbath is more than a useful social convention. It commemorates the creation story in Genesis, when God brought into being his supreme achievement, humanity, on the sixth day and rested on the seventh. It is interesting that the privilege of the Sabbath is not confined to the Hebrew people. It applies also to the "sojourner who is within your gates" (20:10) and even to a person's livestock. All creation is invited to celebrate.

One commandment is not concerned with overt acts: " 'You shall not covet . . .' " (20:17). We are not to be envious of someone's house, wife, ox, or anything else. Now envy is a very real thing to the person experiencing its assaults, but it may not be visible on his face. Thus the man who fantasizes about his neighbor's wife and hates him for having her may appear to be a calm person, civil in his relations with the husband. However, if he continues to covet he may move from thought to action and try to woo the wife away.

With the commandment "You shall not covet," we move into the realm of psychology. In a way rare in the Old Testament, the emphasis is on a state of mind rather than deeds. The commandment is a step toward the inwardness of the New Testament where lustful thoughts are equated with actual adultery.

Interpreted in one way, "You shall not covet" could be the slogan of the rich and comfortable—a warning to the dispossessed to be content with the modest station in which it has pleased God to place them. The answer is to see the Bible as a whole. I must not covet my neighbor's wife or his ox, but I am not commanded to acquiesce in an unjust society. The Bible is full of specific provisions for social justice. The overall command to love your neighbor as yourself concerns more than benevolent feelings. It involves action. It guarantees gleaning rights to the poor; it forbids usury; it makes countless provisions for the welfare and dignity of widows and orphans as well as the "stranger within your gates." Most startling of all, the Bible provides for a fresh start every fifty years—the Jubilee year—when slaves are liberated and mortgaged property returned to the original owners. It is no accident that the Bible has proved to be a very subversive book.

The Ten Commandments are the foundation, but many details need to be filled in. No sooner has God given the Commandments than he issues page after page of supplementary instructions to deal with situations not already explicitly covered. These, as we saw when we looked at Leviticus, are an unclassified mass of regulations. For example, in chapter 21 of Exodus, there are provisions governing, among other things: what to do when a Hebrew slave gets married and is later liberated; what to do with a female slave if her master is not pleased with her; different degrees of homicide; how to punish an ox that gores someone to death; the penalty for leaving a pit uncovered. Page after page it goes on, spelling out the small print of a just society. For instance, there is a strong social ethic in Exodus 23:1-11:

> "You shall not utter a false report. You shall not join hands with a wicked man, to be a malicious witness. You shall not follow a multitude to do evil; nor shall you bear witness in a suit, turning aside after a multitude, so as to pervert justice; nor shall you be partial to a poor man in his suit.
>
> "If you meet your enemy's ox or his ass going astray, you shall bring it back to him. If you see the ass of one who hates you lying under its burden, you shall refrain from leaving him with it, you shall help him to lift it up.
>
> "You shall not pervert the justice due to your poor in his suit. Keep far from a false charge, and do not slay the innocent and righteous, for I will not acquit the wicked. And you shall take no bribe, for a bribe blinds the officials, and subverts the cause of those who are in the right.
>
> "You shall not oppress a stranger; you know the heart of a stranger, for you were strangers in the land of Egypt.
>
> "For six years you shall sow your land and gather in its yield;

but the seventh year you shall let it rest and lie fallow, that the poor of your people may eat; and what they leave the wild beasts may eat. You shall do likewise with your vineyard, and with your olive orchard."

The Old Testament indeed commands us to love our neighbor as ourself. But that command alone provides little guidance for the specific situations in which we constantly have to make decisions. The moral guidelines of the Old Testament, which proliferated with the passage of time, may seem legalistic, even nitpicking. At the same time they are so detailed that a complete way of life can be deduced by putting all its commandments and precepts together, which is what the Hebrews gradually did.

After the staggering events at Sinai, it might seem that the Hebrews have a clear path before them. Instead, decades of wandering in the wilderness stretch ahead, and there are constant problems of morale. In retrospect, Egypt looks not half bad.

The religion of Yahweh is so uncompromising that the Hebrews begin to yearn for easier-going gods. When Moses delays in coming down from the mountain, the people plead with Aaron to make them gods of a more tangible sort. He consents, collecting their jewelry and fashioning a golden calf to which the people offer sacrifices as they proclaim (Exodus 32:4): " 'These are your gods, O Israel, who brought you up out of the land of Egypt!' " It requires all of Moses' persuasive powers to convince Yahweh that he ought not exterminate the apostates.

Finally, there comes the conquest of Canaan. This is a slow process, initially led by Joshua after Moses' death. Probably it covered a period of several centuries. Eventually the land is in the hands of the Hebrews, and their national life in their own homeland can begin. It is not to be a peaceful one. The nation is located on the route between the two great power centers of that part of the world: Egypt and the Mesopotamian area. Constantly the Hebrews find themselves between the anvil and the hammer. They are forced into complex diplomatic and military moves to avoid defeat and assimilation. Their homeland indeed flows with milk and honey, but offers no guarantee of peace and tranquility.

The Hebrews, in the course of consolidating their hold on Canaan, find that their old loosely jointed system of government—depending on charismatic "judges"—is not suited for a nation that has to hold its own with the other powers of the area. They demand a king who can provide stronger leadership. Their first one, Saul, is a brilliant military leader, but subject to acute manic-depressive periods. After a splendid start he loses his grip on the course of events. His successor, David, is by contrast a well-balanced person. He has great skill in winning the support of the people, as well as excelling in the necessary arts of war. He makes so deep an impression on the Hebrews that subsequently, in their darkest hours, they dream of another David on the throne, an "anointed one" (messiah) who would usher in the long deferred time of peace and prosperity.

David's successor is Solomon, a great lover of ostentation and luxury, who creates a "modern state" by his encouragement of trade and his lavish expenditures on public projects, such as his palace and the Temple. He puts the Hebrews on the map, but at a frightful price. Taxes pile up, forced labor is employed by the government. The average person, while perhaps admiring the glory of Solomon's reign, nurses resentments. The Hebrews that settled in the north are particularly alienated from the king. After Solomon's death they break away and form a separate nation, called Israel. In subsequent centuries this state is sometimes allied with the southern remnant, Judah, sometimes at war with it. Finally, the great Assyrian juggernaut in the eighth century ends its independence, deporting many of its people to scattered areas in the empire. They gradually lose their identity in the great melting pot. So only little Judah is left. If the covenant with Yahweh is to be fulfilled, Judah must play the role of the "saving remnant," a concept that figures increasingly in the thought of the southern people during these troubled and often chaotic centuries.

The two kingdoms have a succession of kings, most of whom—according to the biblical accounts—are deplorable. The standard by which they are judged in the Bible is not primarily military or political success, but fidelity to the Sinai covenant. Most of them compromise with the Canaanite religion which has deeply infiltrated the austerity of the Hebrew faith. The kings must try to rule a country in which the two religions are mingled in a way that blurs the distinctiveness of the Hebrew covenant. Thus it is that the Books of Kings and Chronicles find very little to praise in the successors of Solomon.

In the sixth century B.C. it comes the turn of the southern kingdom to be uprooted and incorporated into another great empire, Babylonia this time. The Temple, where the religious life of the Hebrews is centered, is destroyed. Large numbers of people—especially the upper class and leaders—are deported to Babylon. There they remain for several generations. Many are absorbed through intermarriage and a gradual drift toward the religion of their neighbors. But there is a remnant within this remnant that never abandons the covenant nor the hope of return to Jerusalem. It is during this exile that the greatest survival institution of the Hebrews is invented—the synagogue. Deprived of their Temple and its elaborate system of festivals and animal sacrifices, they begin meeting wherever they are for teaching and prayer. The synagogue is destined to serve the Hebrews well in all their subsequent exiles.

The period of exile in Babylonia is not, in many ways, too horrible an experience. There is ample opportunity for the Hebrews to learn practical skills and climb the socioeconomic ladder. Many of the Hebrews drift into interfaith marriages and a syncretic religion.

Meanwhile the Babylonian empire passes into the hands of the Persians, who are by any standard a remarkably tolerant and enlightened people. The emperor sees to it that the various ethnic groups of his crazy-quilt empire are represented at court, and that local cults and customs are not merely tolerated but encouraged. It is a Persian emperor who finally gives permission for those Hebrews who wish to do so to return to Jerusalem and restore the Temple. The difficulties of this task are described in the Books of Nehemiah and Ezra. Many of the Hebrews who never left Jerusalem have married gentile wives. Everything distinctive about the Hebrew people and their religion is being rapidly eroded. The returning Hebrews are, by a process of self-selection, those who have held fast to their faith and are determined to make Jerusalem once more a city where the Sinai covenant is the center of their common life. They succeed, but at a fearful social cost, when many men married to foreign women feel obliged to divorce them and renounce their children.

It is at this stage that one detects a fortress mentality developing among the Hebrews who are still faithful to their covenant. They dare not have too close a contact with gentiles, for this seems invariably to result in religious syncretism. And they are not willing to say, "After all, Yahweh and Baal are both symbols of one ultimate reality." Yahweh was the Lord God, Baal was an idol made with human hands. If Ezra had been reminded that Ruth wholeheartedly embraced the religion of her adopted land, he would surely have insisted that while this was always a possibility, it was statistically improbable in any given case.

This all too brief history of the Hebrew people in the Old Testament times draws to an end. The horrors of military occupation are not over. A Greek-speaking army under Alexander the Great conquers the Middle East, including what are today Israel and Jordan. When Alexander dies prematurely, the huge empire is divided among his successors. The condition of the Hebrews varies according to the ruler of the moment. For one brief time they regain independence after a successful rebellion as described in two spirited books in the Apocrypha, I and II Maccabees. But behind the Greeks come the Romans. They allow the conquered province some autonomy and a fair amount of religious freedom, while keeping their legions always in readiness to suppress any revolts by this traditionally unpredictable nation of Yahweh-worshipers. But at this point we are moving prematurely into the period covered by the New Testament.

⁂ 23 ⁂

The Voice of the Prophets
(Act Two, continued)

How were the Hebrews shaped during the long centuries between their escape from Egypt and the end of the Old Testament period? First of all, by their priests, who were responsible for maintaining the rituals and ethical standards of their religion and safeguarding them from contamination by paganism. Theirs was a quiet, never-ending, day-by-day activity, sometimes well done, sometimes sloppily, but at all times vital for the people's understanding of their relation individually and collectively with their God.

They were shaped also by their rulers. These were first the charismatic judges, later the kings. The latter must be given much credit for fostering a sense of nationhood—though if we can believe the men who wrote the historical books of the Bible, most of the kings were religious and moral disasters.

The most profound shaping influence was the prophets, a word which in Hebrew means "spokesman." These were men who felt themselves called by God to speak his thoughts and judgments. Typically they assumed this role not from any desire for it, but because they were confronted by God and put to work. A classical instance of this kind of encounter is Isaiah's vision of the Lord in the Temple (Isaiah 6:1-8*):

> In the year that King Uzziah died I saw the Lord sitting upon a throne, high and lifted up; and his train filled the temple. Above him stood the seraphim; each had six wings: with two he covered his face, and with two he covered his feet, and with two he flew. And one called to another and said:
>
> "Holy, holy, holy is the LORD of hosts;
> the whole earth is full of his glory."

---

* Biblical quotations in this chapter are from the Revised Standard Version.

And the foundations of the thresholds shook at the voice of him who called, and the house was filled with smoke. And I said: "Woe is me! For I am lost; for I am a man of unclean lips; for my eyes have seen the King, the LORD of hosts!"

Then flew one of the seraphim to me, having in his hand a burning coal which he had taken with tongs from the altar. And he touched my mouth, and said: "Behold, this has touched your lips; your guilt is taken away and your sin forgiven." And I heard the voice of the Lord saying, "Whom shall I send, and who will go for us?" Then I said, "Here I am! Send me."

The beginnings of prophecy are enveloped in the mists of antiquity. By orthodox Jews, Moses is traditionally considered the first prophet. More typical in early times were ecstatic visionaries, working themselves up into a frenzy, like modern whirling dervishes. Closer to the ultimate understanding of the prophet's role was Samuel (eleventh century B.C.), though he was also a judge and combined religious and secular roles.

In the ninth century B.C. we have the mysterious Elijah, who finally disappears in a chariot of fire that has inspired flying saucer speculations. But it is in the eighth century B.C. that the prophets most clearly emerge as the shapers of the Hebrew understanding of history. In this century are Amos, Hosea, and "first Isaiah." Among the prophets arising in the sixth and seventh centuries are Ezekiel, "Second Isaiah," and Jeremiah. The prophetic movement continues with gradually diminishing vigor into post-exilic times. Christians see in John the Baptist a revival of the impulse.

There is not space in this brief book to discuss all the prophets. The reader who wishes to make a start might well begin with Amos, Hosea, and Isaiah. He will quickly enough discover—as is characteristic of the Old Testament—that the "sacred" and the "secular" are inextricably mingled. One moment a prophet finds himself dealing with religious syncretism and uttering appeals for strict fidelity to the Sinai covenant. The next moment he may speak like a president's special adviser, discussing the intricacies of foreign policy and trying to express the will of God in political and military matters. Abruptly he turns to society and its evils, and issues a stirring call for the creation of a more just society. Some prophets will emphasize one thing, others something else, but the reader is more struck by the basic similarities than the differences. On the whole, while not denying the importance of the Temple cult, the prophets are more concerned with social justice than burnt offerings.

Central to the vision of the prophets is the conviction that God reveals himself through the great movements of history. These movements are not arbitrary or chancy; there is cause and effect. The nation that lives by God's laws will prosper. Rain will fall in the right amount, crops will flourish, foreign nations will not come and conquer. But the prophets looked at the actual course of history, and usually found the Hebrew nation in dire peril of moral collapse or threatened by some vast empire on the march. This raised the disturbing question: Why did God permit this? The only answer—if indeed God rewards good nations and punishes bad ones—is that the Hebrew nation is bad. In one way or another it is disregarding the will of God. This might be through social injustice or a reversion to paganism. The task of the prophet is simply to analyze the situation, warn of God's impending wrath, and to propose a cleansing of the nation's life. Then there can be reconciliation between God and nation.

Prophets could be from any background. Jeremiah was a country gentleman. Amos was a herdsman of sheep and goats and a tender of fig trees. He came from the southern kingdom, but directed his message mainly to the northern kingdom. He had a particularly passionate hatred of social injustice. As he observes the luxury of the idle rich, he warns them (Amos 6:4–7):

"Woe to those who lie upon beds of ivory,
    and stretch themselves upon their couches,
and eat lambs from the flock,
    and calves from the midst of the stall;
who sing idle songs to the sound of the harp,
    and like David invent for themselves instruments of music;
who drink wine in bowls,
    and anoint themselves with the finest oils,
    but are not grieved over the ruin of Joseph!

> Therefore they shall now be the first of those to go into exile,
>   and the revelry of those who stretch themselves shall pass
>   away."

Amos does not restrict his warnings to the Hebrew people. In fact, he begins his book with a series of addresses to neighboring lands, pronouncing the judgments of God, precisely as though they too had entered into a covenant relation with him. The scope of God's revelation is becoming worldwide.

Like all the prophets, Amos is aware of the great political and military events all about him, and relates his teaching to specific crises. He lived at the time of the Assyrian threat and accurately prophesied the fall of Israel.

If Amos is the prophet of justice, Hosea is the prophet of love and mercy. By the circumstances of his life—or perhaps through the inspiration of his imagination—he found a perfect symbol for the relation of God and his people. God is the faithful husband, agonizing over his wayward wife, yearning for the day when she will repent and return to his hearth. He has had to chastise her severely, but only out of love, and the hope that she will come to her senses and see where her true happiness resides.

The poetic and religious climax of the prophetic movement is reached with Isaiah. Or, to be more exact, with First Isaiah and Second Isaiah. The Book of Isaiah was composed by at least three prophets: the historical Isaiah (chapters 1 through 39), Second Isaiah (chapters 40 through 55), and Third Isaiah (the remainder of the book). The historical Isaiah was an eighth century B.C. contemporary of Amos and Hosea, at the time of the Assyrian threat. Second Isaiah lived in the sixth century B.C. during the Babylonian captivity. Third Isaiah, the least interesting of the three, dates from the return to Jerusalem at the time of Nehemiah.

First Isaiah, who served as a counselor to the king, believed with passionate intensity that good could come from the Assyrian menace. God was using the pagans as his rod, to chastise his disobedient and corrupt people, but ultimately they would turn to him and reestablish right relations. Jerusalem would not fall. With this conviction, First Isaiah warned against dabbling in power politics; once the Hebrews had turned to God, their safety and survival would be assured. In this particular crisis, Isaiah was proved to be right. Though the northern kingdom fell, as he had predicted, the Assyrian army mysteriously withdrew at the last moment from its siege of Jerusalem.

It was First Isaiah who clearly formulated the concept of the "saving remnant." In Isaiah 10:20-22 he predicts: "In that day the remnant of Israel and the survivors of the house of Jacob will no more lean upon him that smote them, but will lean upon the Holy One of Israel, in truth. A remnant will return, the remnant of Jacob, to the mighty God. For though your people Israel be as the sand of the sea, only a remnant of them will return."

First and Second Isaiah are of particular interest to Christians, because of passages that in retrospect seem to point toward the coming of Christ. For instance, Isaiah 9:6-7:

> For to us a child is born,
>   to us a son is given;
> and the government will be upon his shoulder,
>   and his name will be called
> "Wonderful Counselor, Mighty God,
>   Everlasting Father, Prince of Peace."
> Of the increase of his government and of peace
>   there will be no end,
> upon the throne of David, and over his kingdom,
>   to establish it, and to uphold it
> with justice and with righteousness
>   from this time forth and for evermore.
> The zeal of the LORD of hosts will do this.

In Isaiah 53:4-10, Second Isaiah writes of a suffering servant in a passage that Christians inevitably apply to Christ:

> Surely he has borne our griefs
>   and carried our sorrows;
> yet we esteemed him stricken,
>   smitten by God, and afflicted.
> But he was wounded for our transgressions,
>   he was bruised for our iniquities;
> upon him was the chastisement that made us whole,

and with his stripes we are healed.
All we like sheep have gone astray;
    we have turned every one to his own way;
and the LORD has laid on him
    the iniquity of us all.

He was oppressed, and he was afflicted,
    yet he opened not his mouth;
like a lamb that is led to the slaughter,
and like a sheep that before its shearers is dumb,
    so he opened not his mouth.
By oppression and judgment he was taken away;
    and as for his generation, who considered
that he was cut off out of the land of the living,
    stricken for the transgression of my people?
And they made his grave with the wicked
    and with a rich man in his death,
although he had done no violence,
    and there was no deceit in his mouth.

Yet it was the will of the LORD to bruise him;
    he has put him to grief;
when he makes himself an offering for sin,
    he shall see his offspring, he shall prolong his days;
the will of the LORD shall prosper in his hand . . .

It may be stretching things too far to insist that these two
Isaiahs had a clear foreknowledge of the eventual coming of
Christ. Both were probably speaking in the framework of traditional messianic hopes, though with a dawning understanding
that the Messiah might be one called upon to suffer as well as
to triumph. Still, these passages do suggest that the religious
intuitions of the first two Isaiahs were evolving in a direction
that eventually would make it possible for people to recognize
in Jesus of Nazareth the suffering servant of Second Isaiah.

We have seen from this sampling of prophets how they
shaped the way the Hebrew people understood their destiny.
This shaping influence is to be seen everywhere in the Bible.
The historical books are not *merely* history. They are interpreted history. Thus it is that the biblical authors are never content
simply to recount events. Over long periods of time their annals are edited and re-edited, not to change the events, but to

bring to bear upon them the kind of understanding of the course of history that the prophets made available. The insights of the prophets become the glasses through which the Hebrews view their nation's special history and each individual's relation to that history.

⟫ 24 ⟪
Darkening Questions
(Act Two, concluded)

In the last few centuries before the time of Christ, the prophetic movement seems to have spent its strength. Prophets appear less often; life goes on from one national crisis to another. First the Babylonians, then the Persians, then the Greeks, and finally the Romans almost absentmindedly round out their empires by establishing control over little Judah.

The vision of the special covenant with God never dies. But with each century, it becomes harder to believe that the happy days of King David will soon be restored. More and more the people are driven to a survival strategy. They develop institutions, such as the synagogue, that can assure their future identity, no matter what humiliations they suffer from their powerful neighbors.

The return from Babylon marks a new phase in the life of the Jewish people. It has been a close thing. The practical advantages of living in prosperous and technologically advanced Babylon have seduced many of the people deported there. By no means all of them return to Judah when the tolerant Persians give them the option. The new community at Jerusalem is a remnant of a remnant.

In the Books of Ezra and Nehemiah we see the returning

Jews struggling against desperate odds to recreate a sense of solidarity with those Jews who had been allowed to remain in Jerusalem during the exile. Inevitably, they have to emphasize everything that is most distinctive about their tradition. The observance of the Torah, the kosher laws, the pressures against interfaith marriage all work to strengthen the psychological fortress.

The period between the return from exile and the birth of Jesus is one of deepening questions. It seems as though the nation has tried everything and nothing has succeeded. It has heard the messages of the prophets and has at times made a sincere attempt to live up to the Sinai covenant. It has attempted periodic reformations of its religious and social life. It has tried to look out for its own safety by playing the grim game of power politics in a world where little nations are like small mammals at the feet of dinosaurs. And still the Messiah has not come.

The concept of the Messiah gradually develops in different directions. Originally, he was to be a kind of idealized King David, who would restore independence to the nation and foster devotion to the Sinai convenant. As time went on, some strands of prophetic thought began to broaden out this hope and anticipate a world in which the Messiah reigns, under God, over all peoples. Other writers (as in Daniel 12) emphasize the supernatural character of the final deliverance.

In the closing centuries of the Old Testament period, it must have been difficult to maintain the healthy optimism that the Hebrews experienced when they took possession of Canaan. The world had meanwhile darkened. Nothing worked. Many times the Hebrews must have asked themselves: Is this what it means to be a chosen people?

No wonder if they began to question the old healthy-minded assurance that virtue—on the part of a nation or an individual—will automatically be rewarded, and sin punished. They saw wicked men dying peacefully in bed, surrounded by adoring friends and relatives, and good men dispossessed and treated shamefully. Nor did conventional theories of reward and punishment work well on the international scale. The prophets were kept busy explaining why Yahweh does not always intervene to save his chosen people.

All this adds up to a deepening mood of pessimism and questioning. We saw a sample of it earlier when we looked at the Book of Ecclesiastes. The Preacher simply finds that the traditional assumptions do not work. His ethical grandeur is such that he still chooses to keep the commandments of God, without demanding or expecting that he will be patted on the head by a divine hand.

The same problem is treated—but with far more agony and passion—in the Book of Job, where an ancient folktale is reshaped to dramatize the question: Is God always just in his dealings with individual mortals? The date of the book is uncertain; perhaps during the troubled period of the Babylonian captivity or shortly after the return from exile.

This book is a literary—and moral—high point of the Bible. The plot is simple enough. Up to now, Job has been fortunate in all the circumstances of his life. He is so preeminently virtuous that God, when conversing with Satan, singles him out as an ideal man. Satan is not impressed. He maintains that Job's virtues are a sunny weather kind, and that if misfortune strikes he will turn from God. The latter authorizes Satan to bring afflictions upon Job, to test the steadfastness of his virtuous life.

Everything begins happening. Job's livestock is stolen; his servants are murdered; his children are killed by a wind storm. As though this is not enough, Satan afflicts him with sores from foot to head. Job's wife has endured all she can (Job 2:9–10*): " 'Do you still hold fast your integrity? Curse God, and die.' " But Job is faithful to God: " 'You speak as one of the foolish women would speak. Shall we receive good at the hand of God, and shall we not receive evil?' "

Job's greatest ordeal is when three of his friends come to comfort him. For seven days they sit staring at him, until at last he begins his bitter tirade against the day of his birth. The friends want to help, but they can only insist that he must be very wicked, otherwise these afflictions would not have come

---

* Biblical quotations in this chapter are from the Revised Standard Version.

upon him. His suffering is prima facie evidence of his sins. As Eliphaz puts it (Job 4:7–9):

> "Think now, who that was innocent ever perished?
>   Or where were the upright cut off?
> As I have seen, those who plow iniquity
>   and sow trouble reap the same.
> By the breath of God they perish,
>   and by the blast of his anger they are consumed."

But Job cannot accept this. *He knows* he has lived a decent and obedient life, and he is not going to confess imaginary sins. He begins to sound like the Preacher of Ecclesiastes (Job 12:2–6):

> "No doubt you are the people,
>   and wisdom will die with you.
> But I have understanding as well as you;
>   I am not inferior to you.
>   Who does not know such things as these?
> I am a laughingstock to my friends;
>   I, who called upon God and he answered me,
>   a just and blameless man, am a laughingstock.
> In the thought of one who is at ease there is
>   contempt for misfortune;
>   it is ready for those whose feet slip.
> The tents of robbers are at peace,
>   and those who provoke God are secure,
>   who bring their god in their hand."

Job desperately wants to continue believing that God is just. He implores God to speak to him and explain his afflictions. And suddenly God appears out of a whirlwind and addresses to Job a series of imperious questions: Where was Job when the world was created? Does he send rain upon the earth? Can he secure prey for the lion? Will the wild ox obey him? Did he create the horse? Can he draw a crocodile ashore with a cord?

Now the interesting thing about these questions is that they still leave unexplained the afflictions of Job. But he finds that his questions have been engulfed by the actual presence of God and the vision of his majesty. Job may never know why he has suffered, but he sees his torment in another context now. It is no longer the central fact of his life. The grandeur of God reduces everything else to manageable size. Job's repentance will be not for complaining about his miseries, but for being so centered on himself that he was blind to the glory of his creator. If there is some meaning to his afflictions, it must lie deep in the divine mystery. He says to the Lord (Job 42:2–6):

> "I know that thou canst do all things,
>   and that no purpose of thine can be thwarted.
> 'Who is this that hides counsel without knowledge?'
> Therefore I have uttered what I did not understand,
>   things too wonderful for me, which I did not know.
> 'Hear, and I will speak;
>   I will question you, and you declare to me.'
> I had heard of thee by the hearing of the ear,
>   but now my eye sees thee;
> therefore I despise myself,
>   and repent in dust and ashes."

After the towering words and thoughts that here reach their climax, it comes as a letdown to read the rest of chapter 42 and discover a flat "happy ending" that was probably appended by some later author to reaffirm the simple concept of virtue and reward. We see Job once more prosperous, his children restored to him. And, since he is a virtuous man, he lives to the age of one hundred forty.

The main part of Job is on a completely different level, and is calculated to make anyone abandon a simple causality. Indeed, meditation on it may make it possible to imagine a man put to a shameful death and the day of the event being called by subsequent generations "good."

Over the centuries, and here and there, a new intuition was growing. Only a miracle could resolve the dilemmas of individual and national existence. God, who in earlier times had liberated a slave people by the power of his will, must enter history again in some way even more profound and give humanity a fresh start.

The poets say these things better. In his Christmas Oratorio,

W. H. Auden presents the scene as the chorus of pilgrim people cry out for a miracle:*

Alone, alone, about a dreadful wood
Of conscious evil runs a lost mankind,
Dreading to find its Father lest it find
The Goodness it has dreaded is not good:
Alone, alone, about our dreadful wood.

Where is that Law for which we broke our own,
Where now that Justice for which Flesh resigned
Her hereditary right to passion, Mind
His will to absolute power? Gone. Gone.
Where is that Law for which we broke our own?

The Pilgrim Way has led to the Abyss.
Was it to meet such grinning evidence
We left our richly odoured ignorance?
Was the triumphant answer to be this?
The Pilgrim Way has led to the Abyss.

We who must die demand a miracle.
How could the Eternal do a temporal act,
The Infinite become a finite fact?
Nothing can save us that is possible:
We who must die demand a miracle.

---

* W. H. Auden, "For the Time Being," from *Collected Poems of W. H. Auden,* edited by Edward Mendelson. Copyright 1944 and renewed 1972 by W. H. Auden. Reprinted by permission of Random House, Inc., and Faber and Faber, Ltd.

⋙ 25 ⋘
The Unexpected Good News
(Act Three)

And so the curtain falls on Act Two. The middle—and central—act of the five-act play is ready to be enacted.

The New Testament came into existence by a slow process of accretion and evolution, just as the Old Testament did earlier. The first Christians already had the Old Testament for their scriptures. When they began writing short books about the life of Jesus or the problems of the young Church, they may not have known that they were creating what later generations would also consider Holy Scripture.

In its final form, the New Testament consists of (1) the four gospels; (2) the Book of Acts, a history of the early Church and in particular of Paul's missionary work; (3) assorted letters from church leaders; (4) that strange book Revelation, which purports to look into the future and report the ultimate culmination of history.

John's gospel stands apart in tone and emphasis. The three synoptic gospels—Matthew, Mark, and Luke—have internal connections that are still being studied and debated by scholars. The most common theory is that Mark is the earliest, and that Matthew and Luke used material from it, as well as drawing upon a collection of Jesus' sayings (no longer in existence) and perhaps other sources of information. It is not certain that the authors to whom the gospels are traditionally attributed actually wrote them, though there is general agreement that Luke composed the gospel bearing his name, as well as the Book of Acts.

The difficult question arises as to which gospel this book should concentrate on. A good case could be made for Mark, which is stripped down and terse. A much fuller gospel is Matthew, rich in the teachings of Jesus. Luke has a particularly human quality about it and a wealth of parables. On the whole, Luke seems the best place to begin. Later I shall discuss John's very different gospel.

A word of warning. We are tempted to read the gospels as short biographies of Jesus. If we do, we are soon puzzled and confused. None of the gospels will tell us much of his life between his babyhood and the beginning of his public ministry. Evidently, the men who composed the gospels were interested mainly in what Jesus taught and most of all in the meaning of his death and resurrection.

We saw that the Old Testament period came to an end on a note of discouragement. The bright dream that reached back to Sinai and even to Father Abraham seemed dimmed; a feeling of helplessness gripped many people. In the first two chapters of Luke, the reader is plunged into a different world: soaring hopes and joy. The rustle of the supernatural is everywhere. New life is bursting forth.

This is literally true, for the story centers around two babies. Luke begins with an aged couple, Zechariah and Elizabeth, who have long wanted children. While performing his priestly functions in the Temple, Zechariah suddenly sees the angel Gabriel, who reveals to him that his wife will become pregnant. It is like the story of Abraham and Sarah all over again.

Gabriel next goes to Nazareth and tells a young woman, Mary, who is betrothed to Joseph, a carpenter and descendant of David, that she will conceive and give birth to a son, Jesus, who will reign forever. She reasonably asks how this can be, seeing that she is a virgin. Gabriel assures her (Luke 1:35–37*): " 'The Holy Spirit will overshadow you. So the holy one to be born will be called the Son of God. Even Elizabeth your relative is going to have a child in her old age, and she who was said to be barren is in her sixth month. For nothing is impossible with God.' " Mary needs no more reassurance. She quietly consents to cooperate with God's plans.

Mary goes on a visit to Elizabeth, and when she enters the

---

*Biblical quotations in this chapter are from the New International Version.

room unborn John leaps in the womb. It is "for joy," Elizabeth explains. And indeed, if one wanted a single word to express the mood of these first two chapters of Luke, joy is the word. A new age is beginning.

Caught up in the drama of salvation, Mary sings what was later called the Magnificat (Luke 1:46–55):

"My soul praises the Lord
  and my spirit rejoices in God my Savior,
for he has been mindful of the humble state of his servant.
From now on all generations will call me blessed,
  for the Mighty One has done great things for me—
  holy is his name.
His mercy extends to those who fear him,
  from generation to generation.
He has performed mighty deeds with his arm;
  he has scattered those who are proud in their inmost thoughts.
He has brought down rulers from their thrones
  but has lifted up the humble.
He has filled the hungry with good things
  but has sent the rich away empty.
He has helped his servant Israel,
  remembering to be merciful
to Abraham and his descendants forever,
  even as he said to our fathers."

After the birth of John, his father sings a song of rejoicing, prophesying the future role of his son as a forerunner who will prepare the way of the Lord.

The second chapter begins with secular history. The Roman overlords have decided to register everyone so that taxes can be imposed. Joseph and Mary journey to Bethlehem for the registration. While there, her time comes upon her, and since the inns are full, the baby is born in a manger.

This is no ordinary birth. Shepherds out in the dark fields suddenly see an angel, bringing them the news that a savior has been born in Bethlehem. All at once a heavenly choir sings the Gloria, and the angels disappear as quickly as they had come. The bewildered shepherds journey to Bethlehem. It is just as they have been told: a baby lying in a manger. They go away, telling their story far and wide. Meanwhile Mary stores up these memories.

Everywhere the baby Jesus is taken there are those who lift their voices in praise. When he is presented in the Temple in accordance with ancient custom, an old man named Simeon— who has been told by the Holy Spirit that he will live to see the Messiah—picks up the child in his arms and expresses his vision of Jesus' future (Luke 2:29–32):

> "Sovereign Lord, as you have promised,
>   you now dismiss your servant in peace.
> For my eyes have seen your salvation,
>   which you have prepared in the sight of all people,
> a light for revelation to the Gentiles and for glory to your people Israel."

Finally, still in chapter 2, the family returns to Nazareth, and we are briefly told (Luke 2:40): "And the child grew and became strong; he was filled with wisdom, and the grace of God was upon him."

When next we hear of Jesus, he is twelve years old, and is in Jerusalem with Joseph and Mary for the Passover. His parents start home, not realizing he has stayed behind. When they discover this, they hasten back and find their son sitting with the teachers and asking questions. All are amazed at his understanding. His mother scolds him for the anxiety he has caused them, but he answers in words that prefigure the future (Luke 2:49): " 'Didn't you know I had to be in my Father's house?' "

The curtain falls on these early scenes. About twenty years later it rises again at the start of John's ministry (chapter 3). From the start, he emphasizes that his task is to prepare the way for one greater than he. He warns the people not to presume on their descent from Father Abraham, and he emphasizes the most basic principles of morality—share with the poor, be honest, don't extort money. He baptizes them as a token of repentance and a cleansed life. But he makes it clear that the one who will come has a far more powerful baptism to offer.

It is during this early ministry of John that Jesus has his first clear summons to a special destiny. As he emerges from baptism he has a vision of the Holy Spirit, in form like a dove, and from the sky a voice proclaims (Luke 3:22): " 'You are my Son, whom I love; with you I am well pleased.' "

In chapter 4 we see Jesus confronting the temptations that face anyone who has resolved to devote his life to the good of other people. The Devil urges him to turn stones into bread, so as to feed the poor; he is offered all the kingdoms of the earth; he is urged to jump unharmed from the pinnacle of the Temple. But Jesus refuses to take advantage of his special relation with God, and the voice of the tempter fades away.

He is now ready to proceed with his ministry. He begins it at the synagogue in his home town of Nazareth, reading the passage from Isaiah which proclaims: " 'The Spirit of the Lord is on me, because he has anointed me/to preach good news to the poor." The initial reaction is friendly, but when he says that no prophet is accepted in his own town, the congregation is infuriated, and tries to throw him off a cliff. He has encountered his first violent opposition, but not his last.

When Jesus begins teaching in Capernaum, the people are "amazed at his teaching, because his message had authority" (Luke 4:32). This is a danger signal. The usual rabbi of his time made his points by searching the Scriptures. Jesus apparently could speak from the depths of his own knowledge. He might bolster his arguments with scriptual passages; just as often he simply said, "but *I* tell you." This was blasphemy or close to it.

In the same chapter we find Jesus healing the sick and driving out the demonic spirits that were thought to cause illness. It is as though the very wellsprings of life were in this man, and the normal healing processes are intensified in his presence.

With chapter 5, he begins to seek followers. First he turns to Simon (Peter) and by a miraculous draft of fish convinces him that he stands in the presence of the numinous. When invited to become a fisher of men, Peter obeys. Another early follower is the tax collector, Levi (Matthew), who obeys a simple "Follow me." His presence among the disciples is of course an affront to the more patriotic people who regarded tax collectors as lackeys of the hated Romans.

Coming to chapter 6, we find Jesus on a collision course with some of the Pharisees. It is important to be fair to the latter. They represented the deepest understanding of the Jewish heritage in their time, and they sought ways to maintain that tradition and make it viable in the context of a country occupied by the pagan Romans. They and Jesus had much in common, but the freedom with which he interpreted the Mosaic law began to disturb them.

Jesus' controversies with the Pharisees often grew out of disagreement over how the Sabbath should be observed. For instance, we find him and his disciples walking through a field on the Sabbath and eating some of the grain. This work, light though it is, clearly violates the Sabbath. Jesus defends himself by pointing out that when David was fleeing from Saul and no common bread was at hand, he ate consecrated bread from the altar. Jesus infuriated the Pharisees still further one Sabbath when he healed a man who had a shriveled hand. Around this time, his adversaries begin discussing amongst themselves what to do about this disturbing rabbi.

Next we find Jesus addresing the problems of organization. He singles out a dozen of his disciples and gives them special responsibilities as apostles. This done, he meets with a large crowd of followers, heals the sick, and pronounces the Beatitudes (a fuller version is found in Matthew 5:3–12). These completely reverse common sense assumptions. The poor, by virtue of being poor, are already in the Kingdom of God; those who weep now are guaranteed laughter later (Luke 6:20–22):

"Blessed are you who are poor,
  for yours is the kingdom of God.
Blessed are you who hunger now,
  for you will be satisfied.
Blessed are you who weep now,
  for you will laugh.
Blessed are you when men hate you,
  when they exclude you and insult you

and reject your name as evil,
  because of the Son of Man."

Not content to leave it at that, Jesus warns the rich in a parallel pronouncement (Luke 6:24-26):

"But woe to you who are rich,
  for you have already received your comfort.
Woe to you who are well fed now,
  for you will go hungry.
Woe to you who laugh now,
  for you will mourn and weep.
Woe to you when all men speak well of you,
  for that is how their fathers treated the false prophets."

We have now looked at the first six chapters, which set the stage for what follows. And we have heard the first faint rumors of the dangers he will soon face. Ordinary people respond to him, but he creates a profound uneasiness in the hearts of many sincerely religious people. They cannot deny his deeds, but they question his loyalty to the Law. Meanwhile, we must imagine the Romans keeping a wary eye on him. He looks peaceful—but could he be secretly plotting a rebellion?

A few more episodes will round out the picture. In chapter 7 the story of the Roman centurion is, first of all, a dramatization of faith. The centurion expects his military commands to be obeyed; he sees in Jesus a person with comparable authority. The second point is that the centurion is a gentile. The doors of the Kindom of God seem to be open for all humanity.

The Pharisees are often attracted to this rabbi, though troubled by the company he keeps. We have the account of a Pharisee who invites Jesus to dinner. A woman with a bad reputation enters the house and anoints his feet with perfume. The Pharisee is disappointed that Jesus does not send her packing. Instead, he tells a parable, the moral of which is "her many sins have been forgiven" (Luke 7:47). Jesus' future darkens a shade more at this point. Only God can forgive sins.

Jesus' message evidently appealed as much to women as to men (see, for instance, Luke 8:1-3). This is true to the end, as we shall discover in the account of the crucifixion. One searches in vain to find in the gospels any trace of condescension on the part of Jesus in his contacts with women. They seemed to have known intuitively that, to use the modern term, he was "liberated."

Most of Jesus' miracles are of the healing type, but there are also some that show power over the normal processes of nature. He calms a fierce storm over a lake, and rebukes his disciples for not having sufficient faith. Then, in chapter 9, he feeds the five thousand by multiplying two fish and a few loaves of bread. It is as though he, the Lord of nature, can accelerate the whole cycle of grain sown, crop harvested, bread baked, or the cycle from fish egg to fish in the net.

Jesus asks his disciples to tell him who the crowds believe him to be. Some mention one of the prophets. Peter speaks up: The Christ of God. Jesus does not deny this, but tells them to keep the secret. He apparently does not want a following that will identify him with the kind of Messiah—a sort of super King David—that the word easily suggests.

More and more frequently, he tells his disciples to prepare for the time when he is no longer visibly with them. In the most serious way possible, he warns them (Luke 9:23–26):

> "If anyone would come after me, he must deny himself and take up his cross daily and follow me. For whoever wants to save his life will lose it, but whoever loses his life for me will save it. What good is it for a man to gain the whole world, and yet lose or forfeit his very self? If anyone is ashamed of me and my words, the Son of Man will be ashamed of him when he comes in his glory and in the glory of the Father and of the holy angels."

It is a few days later that Jesus takes Peter, John, and James with him to a mountain top. While he is praying, his garments suddenly gleam, and Moses and Elijah appear, telling him about his approaching death in Jerusalem. Peter, often impulsive and foolish, proposes that they build three shelters for the three men. A voice speaks from a cloud, confirming the voice heard at the time of Jesus' baptism—"This is my son." Abruptly, the vision ends.

Jesus continues his healing and teaching, though often interspersing prophecies of his destiny in Jerusalem. In some ways life goes on as usual. The disciples argue among themselves about which will be greatest in the times to come, and once again Jesus has to remind them that the first will be last and the last first. John is troubled when he sees a man driving out demons in Jesus' name; the fellow isn't "one of us." Jesus replies with brisk practicality that anyone who is not against them is for them. In passing through an unfriendly Samaritan village he has to persuade James and John not to call down fire from heaven.

The same chapter contains the parable of the Good Samaritan. The Samaritans were considered semi-heretics. To single one of them out for praise was equivalent to holding up a Soviet commissar as an exemplar for Americans.

This parable, taken alone, might suggest an activistic ethic. The point is to do something. But Jesus does not always put action first. We have the episode of the two sisters, Mary and Martha. The latter bustles about getting dinner and feeling sorry for herself, because Mary doesn't lift a hand; she is too busy listening to Jesus. In reply to Martha's complaints, Jesus sets the situation in the context of eternity. He gently chides Martha for worrying too much, and says that Mary has made a better choice.

By this time some impression of Jesus' personality begins to emerge. In particular, one senses a hard-nosed realism in his understanding of how human beings function, coupled with a determination to turn daily, fallen human nature upside down. His psychological realism comes out particularly in the parables, which derive their force from an uncannily exact understanding of the human soul. Anyone who has slowed down a bit while driving past an automobile accident, then remembered important duties at the end of the trip and stepped on the gas, will have no trouble understanding the story of the Samaritan and the other passersby.

Meanwhile, there is increasing tension between Jesus on the one hand and the Pharisees and Scribes (experts in the Hebrew Law) on the other. Jesus denounces the Pharisees for concentrating on the tiniest aspects of the Law while neglecting such simple requirements as justice and love. They are like tombs full of decay. One of the Scribes protests that Jesus is insulting them also, and Jesus replies with burning words: " 'And you experts in the law, woe to you, because you load people down with burdens they can hardly carry, and you yourselves will not lift one finger to help them.' " The Pharisees and Scribes are further hardened in their suspicions of Jesus, and are determined to catch him saying something that can bring about his destruction.

Looking back now at the first half of Luke, what strikes us most about Jesus? Perhaps the greatest jolt is how often he says the word *I*. We are used to teachers who say "Follow my advice," but not to those who say "Follow *me*." And with the use of the first-person pronoun go such claims as the ability to forgive sins. We can understand why his enemies thought he was trying to create a blasphemous personality cult.

When we come to his teachings on morality, he reaffirms much of humankind's universal wisdom: Be kind, be honest, and the like. At the same time he turns conventional wisdom upside down, as when he insists that the first shall be last and the last first. We begin to suspect that he is aiming at a profound reorientation of the human soul.

No wonder that Jesus bewildered his followers almost as much as his enemies. Nor has the passage of time made it easier to come to terms with him. Yet—there is no figure from antiquity who is more compellingly *real* than this man. Not even Dante, not even Shakespeare could have created such a character by sheer power of imagination. He stands before us in his complexity and solidity, and we feel a little ghostly and vague.

26

Bad News and Good
(Act Three, continued)

As he prepares for the trip to Jerusalem, Jesus continues to heal and to teach. In chapter 12, he cautions his followers against the Pharisees, whom he calls hypocrites. He assures them that God knows every hair on each person's head. He tells them how to behave if hauled into court, and assures them they need not worry. He warns them not to live for material things; death ends all that.

The recurrent theme is: don't worry. Life can marshal its brutalities against them, but on the deepest level, they are safe. They must trust his promises.

In chapter 13 there is another controversy over the Sabbath. A crippled woman is healed in the synagogue. The synagogue leader plaintively asks why people can't be cured on weekdays. Jesus hurls the charge of hypocrisy and points out that no one hesitates on the Sabbath to water livestock. His detractors are verbally defeated but they store up these episodes for future use.

A conversation with some friendly Pharisees—not all of them by any means are hostile—leads him to think of Jerusalem, the holy city of his people, and he utters a lament over the future destruction of the city (Luke 13:34–35*):

> "O Jerusalem, Jerusalem, you who kill the prophets and stone those sent to you, how often I have longed to gather your children together, as a hen gathers her chicks under her wings, but you were not willing! Look, your house is left to you desolate. I tell you, you will not see me again until you say, 'Blessed is he who comes in the name of the Lord.' "

---

* Biblical quotations in this chapter are from the New International Version.

The theme of the reversal of earthly station is dramatized again in chapter 14 when he advises his disciples to take the lowest seats at a feast, so if the host wishes to move them, it can only be upward. This admonition leads to the account of a rich man who invites many guests to a banquet, and they make every conceivable excuse for not coming. The host then has his servants go out into the street and invite the rabble. But there are still some vacant seats. Finally the host sends his servants again, this time to compel the attendance of those whom they invite. He (like God) will not ultimately be thwarted.

Jesus makes it inescapably clear that there is a price to be paid by those who follow him. He reminds them that if they are going to build a tower, they would get an estimate of the cost before laying the foundations. Or a king would check to see how many soldiers he has before confronting another king in combat. Impulsive, half-hearted commitment will not do.

During the same period, Jesus tells some of his most hopeful parables (chapter 15). These seem designed to put the focus on the individual. One human being who repents is significant enough to set the angels singing with joy. This is illustrated by the parables of the Lost Sheep, the Lost Coin, and the Prodigal Son. The last, as so often in Jesus' teaching, involves a paradox, even an apparent injustice. The wastrel son is welcomed back with a feast; his virtuous older brother has never been so honored. The point, of course, is that the younger boy has been "lost" and his brother has been home all the time and no one had to agonize—and then rejoice—over him.

Chapter 16 is devoted mainly to stewardship. The rich man's manager is shrewd and effective in his job. The message is that disciples of Christ should be similarly efficient in handling the details of their spiritual life. The parable of the rich man and Lazarus, which soon follows, makes it clear that wealth is a peril because of the hardness of heart it so often engenders. The conclusion of the parable has a double meaning, as Jesus thinks of what lies ahead for him (Luke 16:27–31):

> "He [the rich man] answered, 'Then I beg you, father, send Lazarus to my father's house, for I have five brothers. Let him warn them, so that they will not also come to this place of torment.' "

"Abraham replied, 'They have Moses and the Prophets; let them listen to them.' "

" 'No, father Abraham,' he said, 'but if someone from the dead goes to them they will repent.' "

"He said to him, 'If they do not listen to Moses and the Prophets, they will not be convinced even if someone rises from the dead.' "

More and more Jesus talks about the kingdom of God as already existing in principle ("in you"); its visible manifestation will come when least expected. The Son of Man (a term that Jesus applies to himself) will appear while people are going about their usual activities. There will not be time to pack up our belongings before we flee. Of two people in the same bed, one will be taken, the other not.

Chapter 18 illustrates Jesus' particular loathing for self-righteousness. He tells of a Pharisee and a tax collector who happen to be in the Temple at the same time. The Pharisee delivers an encomium on himself. He doesn't rob or commit adultery; most of all, he isn't a tax collector. All the tax collector can do is confess that he is a sinner. But in the eyes of God, the tax collector is the one worthy of mercy. Again we have the theme of the reversal of positions.

One of the most beloved sections of Luke is Jesus' invitation to children (Luke 18:15–17):

People were also bringing babies to Jesus to have him touch them. When the disciples saw this, they rebuked them. But Jesus called the children to him and said, "Let the little children come to me, and do not hinder them, for the kingdom of God belongs to such as these. I tell you the truth, anyone who will not receive the kingdom of God like a little child will never enter it."

This has been the scripture for countless sermons, mostly saccharine, and has encouraged the sentimental belief that a kind of mindless spontaneity is the key to the kingdom of God. Jesus knew better than to treat children with such condescension. One may speculate that what he valued in them was their willingness to follow those that they had reason to trust, such as their parents.

The episode of the rich man who has always obeyed the Law comes next. Jesus, sensing that possessions are a spiritual barrier to this man, bluntly commands him to sell everything he has and give the proceeds to the poor. We can imagine the rich man's face dropping. It has never occurred to him that this ultimate sacrifice would be demanded. Evidently Jesus was convinced that the rich face special obstacles when they aim at the Kingdom of God, though he did not completely rule out the possibility.

The conversation with the rich man is followed by Jesus' warning to the Apostles that he will shortly be put to death. These men do not quite understand. They are still more bewildered when he assures them that on the third day he will rise again. Reading this gospel from the distance of almost two thousand years, it is easy to see how Jesus' thoughts are now in Jerusalem. The shape of a cross is superimposed over all the landscapes of his mind. Increasingly, he sees his death as part of God's plans for bringing into existence the Kingdom of God. He will be revealed as the suffering Messiah whom Isaiah intuitively prophesied.

In chapter 19, Jesus and his disciples are journeying to Jerusalem for the Passover celebration. It is the time of year the Romans particularly dread. Great numbers of Jews from all over the Empire will be there; a frenzied religious and patriotic zeal will be in the air. Mobs can form quickly and dangerously. One can imagine Pontius Pilate conferring with his political and military advisers, bracing himself for the uncertain task of maintaining public order.

Luke, with his eye for human interest details, pauses to relate the story of Zacchaeus. He is a wealthy tax collector who wants to see Jesus, but is so short he has to climb a tree to have a look. Jesus sees him and invites himself to be the tax collector's guest. The crowd is horrified—the idea of dining with a sinner! But Zacchaeus has caught a glimpse of a new way of life. He gives half his possessions to the poor, and offers to pay back fourfold anything he has gained by cheating. (The Romans looked the other way when their foreign tax collectors gathered in more than the amount that had to be given to the

Roman authorities.) Jesus reads the meaning of these actions, and tells the crowd that salvation has come to this man.

Next follows another of Jesus' hard-bitten parables, the one dealing with servants to whom varying amounts of money are entrusted while their master is away. Those handling the most money prove most aggressive in their stewardship. The moral seems to be that talents are to be used, not safeguarded in cold storage.

At last the familiar story of the entry into Jerusalem comes. Jesus sends two of his disciples to borrow a colt. He rides into Jerusalem with people spreading their cloaks before him. The Messiah has come at last! The crowds shout themselves hoarse, proclaiming "the king who comes in the name of the Lord," and "peace in heaven and glory in the highest."

Then comes the cleansing of the Temple, as Jesus drives out the money changers and the sellers of sacrificial doves. "A den of robbers" is what he calls them, probably remembering their high profits. Most of all, he seems affronted at the desecration of the Temple. It was not built to be a marketplace.

It is clear that Jesus is in no mood for a compromise. He has come to Jerusalem to force the issue: people must make up their minds about him, yes or no. His enemies, of course, follow him about, trying to trick him into doing or saying something that will guarantee his doom, but he proves more quick-witted than any of them.

In his parable about the tenants of the vineyard (chapter 20), he tells how a man rents a vineyard to some sharecroppers, who then beat the servant he sends to collect his share of the harvest. He dispatches several other servants who receive similar treatment. Finally, he sends his own son, hoping the tenants will respect him at least. Instead, they murder him. Nothing remains but for the owner to come in person, kill the tenants, and entrust the vineyard to others.

The "teachers of the law and the chief priests" look for a way to arrest him, but for the moment the people are on his side. So they send agents who first pay slavish tribute to his teaching and then ask the seemingly innocuous question: Is it right to pay taxes to Caesar? Whatever he answers will offend someone—the fiercely patriotic Zealots or the brutal Romans. He escapes the trap by a visual parable. Asking to see a coin, he inquires whose likeness and inscription are on it. "Caesar's," the false disciples answer. Jesus then draws the moral—give Caesar what is his, and God what is his. In thus settling the question he could not know that, centuries later, this reply would be a foundation for the doctrine of the separation of church and state.

One has the feeling of a kind of shadowboxing going on at this stage between Jesus and his enemies, each seeking to force the other into a rhetorical corner. But they are not really boxing with shadows. Two irreconcilable forces are locked in mortal combat; it is war to the finish.

In the remaining chapters of Luke the focus is on the events leading to Jesus' death and what happens afterward. Jesus is teaching each day in the Temple; the tensions of the Passover season are steadily mounting. One can imagine the thoughts going through the minds of his enemies. Here is a man who seems to claim some kind of identity with God himself. He forgives sins and plays fast and loose with the Sabbath. He also stirs up the masses by his very presence. The situation may pass out of control. His disciples could turn into a mob and bring upon the nation the wrath of the Romans, with the destrction of the Temple, the city, and a whole way of life. Jesus must have seemed a threat to both the religious and political status quo. Perhaps, his opponents must have thought, he was simply too dangerous a risk to tolerate.

The final scenes leading to Jesus' death begin with chapter 22. Each of the gospels gives substantially the same account. The beginning of the end is the decision of the apostle Judas to cooperate with Jesus' enemies. Why did he do this? Luke can only say that the Devil inspired him. Judas remains a mysterious figure, though many have ingeniously speculated about him. What counts is what he did. He went to the chief priests and offered to betray Jesus. They were delighted and agreed to pay him for his services. From now on Judas is waiting until Jesus is alone, so that he can be arrested without creating a riot.

Next we see Jesus making preparations for the Passover. The

ancient rite is about to be transformed into the sacrament that later will go by such diverse names as the Eucharist, the Mass, the Lord's Supper, and Holy Communion. The sacrifice of animals will be replaced by the one and perfect sacrifice of Jesus (Luke 22:13–20):

> They left and found things just as Jesus had told them. So they prepared the Passover.
>
> When the hour came, Jesus and his apostles reclined at the table. And he said to them, "I have eagerly desired to eat this Passover with you before I suffer. For I tell you, I will not eat it again until it finds fulfillment in the kingdom of God."
>
> After taking the cup, he gave thanks and said, "Take this and divide it among you. For I tell you I will not drink again of the fruit of the vine until the kingdom of God comes."
>
> And he took bread, gave thanks and broke it, and gave it to them, saying, "This is my body given for you; do this in remembrance of me."
>
> In the same way, after the supper he took the cup, saying, "This cup is the new covenant in my blood, which is poured out for you."

A sense of approaching doom pervades the room. Jesus knows that one of his disciples will betray him. They begin speculating about who this could be. Then, at this solemn moment the disciples reveal how superficial their newborn life actually is. Of all things, they resume their old argument about which of them is the greatest. Jesus assures them there will be honor enough for all. Then he turns to Peter and soberly predicts that before a cock crows he will three times deny that he ever knew Jesus.

Now comes the lonely night on the Mount of Olives. When Jesus and his followers arrive there, he withdraws a little distance and prays to be spared the ultimate ordeal. But he concludes, " 'Not my will, but yours be done.' " Soon an armed crowd led by Judas appears. Jesus is led away to the house of the high priest, and Peter watches from a distance. Before the night is over, he three times denies he has ever known this man. A rooster crows. Peter goes outside and weeps uncontrollably.

At dawn Jesus is taken before the Sanhedrin, the council

consisting of both religious and lay leaders which passes on serious questions of the Law and violations of it. They ask whether he is the Christ (Messiah). He prophesies that from now on,
the "Son of Man" will be seated at the right hand of God. They
then ask whether he is the "Son of God" and he does not deny
it. His interrogators are delighted. He has committed an act of
blasphemy. They can pronounce a death sentence on him.

But they cannot carry it out. Not without the consent of the
procurator, Pontius Pilate. And Pilate, like most Romans, is
bored by the endless religious wrangles of the Jews. It is therefore necessary to rephrase the accusation so that Jesus will
seem a menace to the Roman authority. When they bring him
before Pilate they claim that Jesus is teaching that one should
not pay taxes to the Romans and that he claims to be the Messiah, which they translate as "king" for Pilate's benefit.

Pilate questions Jesus briefly and is not impressed by the
charges brought against him. The accusers feel their case slip-
ping away. They shift ground a little and say that this man stirs
up people all over Judea. Pilate still does not seem impressed.
Perhaps he doubts that any group of Jews would have a tender
solicitude for the stability of the Roman regime.

On learning that Jesus is a Galilean, Pilate senses a way out
of his dilemma. Jesus is actually under Herod's jurisdiction.
What more natural and proper than to turn the case over to
Herod? The latter is in Jerusalem at that time, and is delighted
at a chance to see Jesus. Maybe this strange fellow will perform
a miracle. Herod plies him with questions, but Jesus is uncom-
municative. Finally Herod sends him back to Pilate, who summons the accusers and tells them that neither he nor Herod
sees any reason for the death penalty. He will release the prisoner.

The accusers have one last card to play. It is a custom that
each year one prisoner, chosen by the shouts of the populace,
be released. Barabbas, who has been involved in murder and a
rebellion, is the choice of the crowds. When Pilate asks what to
do with Jesus, they shout, "Crucify him!" Pilate, weak-willed
and unwilling to stand by his convictions, is being swept along
by a maneuvered street rabble. The ever-present nightmare is

no doubt in his thoughts: the lively possibility of a riot which would escalate to full-scale revolt.

Finally, Pilate decides to end the whole unpleasant episode by granting the wish of the crowd. He releases Barabbas and confirms the death sentence on Jesus.

As Jesus is led to Golgotha, a large number of his disciples go along, including many women who mourn and weep. He turns to them and tells them not to weep for him, but for themselves and their children when the day of devastation descends upon the city.

Now comes the actual crucifixion at noon. His clothes are divided among the soldiers. Some of his enemies stand by, taunting him—if he is the Messiah, why doesn't he save himself? The Roman soldiers join in the game. Above his head is a sign probably put there by Pilate to mock the Jews: THIS IS THE KING OF THE JEWS. Human nature at its most vicious is abroad this day.

And yet, in the midst of the horror and cruelty, there is a moment of transcendence, when one of the criminals crucified with him somehow senses that Jesus is no common malefactor, and turns to him with some traces of faith. Jesus looks him in the face and promises that this very day the dying criminal will be in paradise.

His enemies do not have long to mock him. Three hours on the cross is a short time, as crucifixions go. In mid-afternoon Jesus cries out, " 'Father, into your hands I commit my spirit,' " and his life ceases. It remains for a Roman centurion, who could not care less about religious controversies, to sum up the day's event: " 'Surely this was a righteous man.' "

The crowds gradually dwindle and drift away, except for Jesus' close disciples, who linger on at a distance. Meanwhile, there is the matter of burial. A member of the Sanhedrin named Joseph, who had opposed the condemnation of Jesus, goes to Pilate and asks for Jesus' body, which he then buries in a rock tomb originally prepared for himself.

So the story ends. Another good man, a new Socrates teaching a higher way of life and put to death by the practical politicians and fearful religious leaders. For awhile, he inspired strangely disturbing visions of a new life, and lifted many people out of themselves into a different order of existence.

So the story seems to end. But there is an epilogue to the story. On Sunday morning a group of Jesus' women followers go to the tomb with spices to prepare the body properly for its long sleep. They find the entrance open, but the body of Jesus is not inside. Two angels suddenly appear and ask why they are looking for the living among the dead. " 'He is not here; he has risen!' " The women carry word to the apostles and other followers. The reaction is skepticism; these are just hysterical women. Peter, however, runs to the tomb and sees the strips of linen in which the body had been wrapped.

Next comes a series of episodes as Jesus suddenly reveals himself when least expected. There is, for instance, the story of the journey to Emmaus, when two disciples are joined by a stranger who interprets for them the scriptural prophecies of Jesus' death and resurrection. Finally they reach the village and the three of them sit down to dinner. He breaks bread and says a grace. At that moment they recognize him—and he immediately disappears.

A little later, after they return to Jerusalem and tell the followers of this experience, Jesus suddenly appears among them. They think he is a ghost. But he is a very substantial ghost. He shows them his wounds and reveals an appetite for broiled fish. Once again, he expounds the Scriptures, seeing in them a foreshadowing of his own death and resurrection. And he commands the disciples to remain in the city until they are filled with power and can witness to what they have seen.

And finally, Jesus takes his disciples to the vicinity of Bethany, blesses them, and abruptly ascends into heaven. This seems not to have left his disciples desolate. Rather, it lifts up their hearts. They return to Jerusalem overflowing with joy, and are continually at the Temple, rendering praises to God.

Thus the Gospel of St. Luke comes full circle. The first two chapters are filled with exultant joy, joy, joy. Then the scene darkens, and reaches pitchblack when the man of Galilee is put to death. But that is not his end. The early outcries of joy at the

time of his birth were not wishful thinking. The story begins
in joy and ends in joy.

But did all this really happen? Perhaps there is a prior question: *Who and what was this man?* It is possible to start with his
most obvious roles and gradually work our way to his more
sweeping claims:

1. He was a great moral teacher, reaffirming the universal
principles of the moral life and bringing to a sharper focus the
Hebrew understanding of those principles. There is hardly any
controversy here.

2. He was a prophet. Mohammed listed Jesus as one of the
great prophets. He was chosen by God to speak to people and
tell them what they needed to know at their time and place.

3. He was the Messiah, the anointed one, God's special agent
to set the world right.

4. He was the adopted son of God. God chose this man to
make him his unique messenger to humankind. When he
speaks, he speaks with the authority of the one who is to him
as a father.

5. He was, quite literally, the Son of God. His earthly career
began when he was born in Bethlehem, but for all ages before
that he had existed, hidden in the splendor of God's majesty,
awaiting the time when his father would send him in human
likeness on a very special mission to the earth.

6. He was, quite literally, the Word of God. (Here we move
from Luke to John.) He was God's creative and redemptive energy at work. He was one with God. (In time, this way of con-
ceiving of Jesus let to the doctrine of the Trinity, according to
which the Godhead is revealed in three manifestations—the
Father, the Son, and the Holy Spirit.)

Words begin to break down at this point. But however inadequate the poor words may be, they point toward Jesus as the
manifestation of the fourth dimension invading the world of
three dimensions. It is as though God is a book written in Japa-
nese and Jesus is the English translation. The Christ is God
made visible, made audible.

Many of the disciples may have advanced step by step from the most modest concepts of Jesus to the most exalted; others stopped at midpoint. Yet others, like Paul, arrived at the most staggering concept in one great leap of faith. The words matter less than the fact—death itself could be no match for this man.

⋙ 27 ⋘

The Fourth Gospel
(Act Three, concluded)

It occurs to me that, for the sake of completeness, I should add one other possible view of Jesus. Could he have been mentally deranged? In our own times there have been instances of men who went about proclaiming their divinity and teaching in the name of the God whom they identified with themselves. One might point to signs of incipient paranoia revealed by Jesus' growing conviction that enemies were around him everywhere. (But of course, they really were, even in the midst of his closest followers!) Perhaps we have the story of a man who had grandiose dreams of remaking the world, and who, when the world did not properly respond, insanely fixed his hopes on some divine intervention that would reveal him as one with God.

One could go along making a case. But even the most convinced unbeliever seldom does. The plain evidence of the Gospels renders it infinitely unlikely. I can remember how, while still a semi-agnostic, I first read the gospels carefully. I expected to find a water-color Jesus, meek and mild, fond of children and lilies, a soulful but impractical soul. I found as much severity as mildness, and certainly no trace of mental instability. I was suddenly confronted with towering strength, unerring insights into the human condition, a wealth of practical common sense as well as soaring dreams for humanity. It was as though I beheld a complete human being for the first time. I was face to face with someone whose sanity was so overwhelming that it was my mental health that might need to be called into question.

No, when we study the Jesus of the gospels, it is he who challenges our psychic condition, not we who pass judgment on his. There is about his character and his way of meeting situations a kind of balance that we never quite attain. He could be hard as nails, gentle as a child's touch. He could predict doom but always hold forth the hope of salvation. Whatever and whoever he was, he did not need to be set straight. He was born with a sanity that terrifies as well as reassures.

The synoptic gospels (Matthew, Mark, Luke) are like the Old Testament in their concrete character. There is not much metaphysical or theological analysis. True, the deeds and words of Jesus often have staggering theological implications, but it is left up to the reader to translate these into the categories of formal theology and philosophy. In short, though these gospels are written in Greek, the habits of thought reflected in them are thoroughly Hebraic. If you had asked an ancient Hebrew, "What is God?" he would not have replied in the words of the *Book of Common Prayer:* "He is everlasting, without body, parts, or passions; of infinite power, wisdom and goodness." Rather, he would have said something like this: "God made the universe and all life; he promised our father Abraham a land to dwell in; he led us out of the Egyptian bondage; he gave us the Ten Commandments at Sinai, and so forth." You would be free to philosophize and theologize about these events, but what would chiefly linger in your mind would be a series of mental pictures, God at work.

The one gospel that stands by itself is John's. It is more explicitly theological than the three others. For this reason many scholars long believed that it was written very much later than the others—perhaps by a couple of centuries. There would have been time for generations of Christians to meditate on the meaning of Jesus, and the author could concentrate on the insights that gradually came. Today, such extreme theories are uncommon. Some scholars now date John as early as Matthew or Luke, and maintain that quite possibly it was actually written by John, the "beloved disciple," or at least is based on his memories. He would have been a young man in Jerusalem at the time of the crucifixion.

If John is actually much earlier than believed until recently, it may also be historically more accurate than many have thought. In some matters of chronology it seems the most plausible of the gospels. But still, granting all these reassessments, it remains true that one reads it less for its historical account than for the peculiarly deep insights that this gospel provides. By comparison, the three others have a rough-and-ready quality about them. John probes deeper and more profoundly. After reading him, one goes back to the synoptic gospels and finds richer implications than were at first apparent.

John consistently pictures Jesus as somehow one with God. Most of the time he does this by using the term Son of God, but in his first chapter he adopts a different strategy, relying on the phrase Word of God. This may have been partly for the benefit of the gentiles, who were already familiar with the term in philosophic discourse. Word is a translation of the Greek *logos,* whose primary meaning is word or reason. But by the time of John its meaning had broadened out so that it could be used to suggest that power which summoned the world into existence, and the purpose lying behind this. In calling Jesus the Word of God, John suggests an identity between them. The Word is God's creative energy, bringing light out of darkness and becoming flesh in the person of Jesus.

The beginning of chapter 1 briefly states John's understanding of Jesus (John 1:1–18*):

> In the beginning was the Word, and the Word was with God, and the Word was God. He was with God in the beginning.
> Through him all things were made; without him nothing was made that has been made. In him was life, and that life was the

---

*Biblical quotations in this chapter are from the New International Version.

light of men. The light shines in the darkness, but the darkness has not understood it.

There came a man who was sent from God; his name was John. He came as a witness to testify concerning that light, so that through him all men might believe. He himself was not the light; he came only as a witness to the light. The true light that gives light to every man was coming into the world.

He was in the world, and though the world was made through him, the world did not recognize him. He came to that which was his own, but his own did not receive him. Yet to all who received him, to those who believed in his name, he gave the right to become children of God—children born not of natural descent, nor of human decision or a husband's will, but born of God.

The Word became flesh and lived for a while among us. We have seen his glory, the glory of the one and only Son, who came from the Father, full of grace and truth.

John testifies concerning him. He cries out, saying, "This was he of whom I said, 'He who comes after me has surpassed me because he was before me.' " From the fullness of his grace we have all received one blessing after another. For the law was given through Moses; grace and truth came through Jesus Christ. No one has ever seen God, but God the only Son, who is at the Father's side, has made him known.

In this brief prologue, which has inspired countless books of commentary, we see John struggling to find a way to express the oneness of God and Jesus. His Jesus is not simply a good teacher, nor even a prophet appointed by God. He is not merely a Messiah. He is God's creative, redemptive activity. There was never a time when he was not; thus the Christ, who has appeared in human form, has always been. The Word was the agent of creation, the light that drives away darkness. When he appeared in human likeness, he was rejected by the power structure. But those who accepted him found their lives transformed. They were no longer merely biological children, but adopted children of God. In the synoptic gospels there are only faint hints of Christ's prior existence before his birth on earth as a human being. In John, that conviction is a dominant motif. John is saying that Heaven became local in the person of Christ. He is saying that the one who journeyed to earth to transform the human condition is the same intelligence and love that spoke the universe into existence. John does not negate the emphases of the other gospels, but he transcends them.

The fourth gospel is relatively sparse in miracles, only seven being recorded. They are carefully selected by John, so that each serves as a kind of parable, illuminating the significance of Jesus. The first of these miracles is at the wedding feast in Cana (John 2:1–11). The wine runs out and Jesus turns water into wine of a better quality than they had been drinking. It has often been pointed out that the quantity was around 120 gallons, surely in excess of any need. But John's purpose in telling the story is to let it symbolize the new wine of the gospel, better than anything they had drunk before.

Throughout this gospel, we find Jesus insisting on his unique relation with God. Frequently he forces the issue—do you believe in me or not? Sometimes he indulges in rather long discourses, as in chapter 5. There was first an episode in which he doubly horrified his enemies by healing on the Sabbath and saying words that made him equal with God. Jesus tries to meet their objections. He pictures himself as doing always what the Father does; as being the giver of new life; as the one to whom the Father has entrusted all judgment. And he adds that anyone who fails to honor the Son fails to honor the Father. Language could hardly go farther. Point by point, he equates himself with God. No wonder he arouses both deep commitment and a wild fury of opposition.

There is no space to discuss John chapter by chapter, but perhaps enough has been said to indicate its special emphasis on Christology—What think ye of Christ? And in his gospel, the claims of Jesus are stated in starker form than in the other gospels. I skip now to the long discourse in chapters 14 through 16, the words of Jesus to his disciples after they have triumphantly entered Jerusalem and he is awaiting his inevitable death. The tone of this discourse can be sensed by singling out some of the statements that Jesus makes: Do not let your hearts be troubled. Trust in God; trust also in me. . . . I am the way and the truth and the life. No one comes to the Father except through me. . . . You may ask me for anything in my name, and I will do it. . . . I will ask the Father, and he will give you another Counselor to be with you forever—the Spirit of truth. . . . He who loves me will be loved by my Father. . . . I do not give to you as the world gives. . . . I am the true vine and my Father is the gardener. . . . Love each other as I have loved you. . . . A time is coming when anyone who kills you will think he is offering a service to God. They will do such things because they have not known the Father or me. . . . When he, the Spirit of truth, comes, he will guide you into all truth. . . . I came from the Father and entered the world; now I am leaving the world and going back to the Father. . . . Take heart! I have overcome the world. . . .

The time for conversation with his disciples is coming to an end. In chapter 17 he prays for himself and for his disciples and all believers. In the following chapter he is arrested, and in the next crucified, and in chapter 20 there is an empty tomb. Meanwhile, the short passages just cited from John's long discourse point to the paradox of Jesus' claims. Nothing could be more absolute than his demands upon his disciples. But at the same time, all commands are enveloped in the radiance and mystery of love. His commands are what love demands.

⇒ 28 ⇐

The Outward Movement (Act Four)

Act Four is the story of what happened after the crucifixion, resurrection, and ascension. The biblical accounts carry us through most of the first century. The new faith evolves and spreads as a result of the missionary movement to which the apostles and many quite ordinary disciples feel called. The old question of whether God is concerned primarily with one people is settled in the course of this work. Christianity emerges as an explicitly universal religion.

The transition between Acts Three and Four is smoothly made by Luke. In the last chapter of his Gospel the disciples behold Jesus ascending to heaven. Overjoyed rather than dispirited, they return to Jerusalem and give thanks in the Temple.

The beginning of the Book of Acts repeats the story of the ascension, and then traces the history of the early Church. It concentrates in particular on the ventures and adventures of that most complex figure of antiquity, Paul. Few books are written with equal vividness. One might read Acts for the sheer drama that enlivens almost every page.

There is not space to cover the whole book, but one can at least single out some of the highpoints, to show the variety and sweep of this amazing chronicle. For instance, in chapter 2 we observe the disciples gathered together, waiting for some new revelation. It is the time of the Jewish Pentecost, a combined harvest celebration and commemoration of the gift of the Law at Sinai. Suddenly there is the sound of a violent wind and they see tongues of fire resting on each person. Filled with the Holy Spirit, they begin speaking in a multitude of tongues. The polyglot crowds standing outside hear the tumult and marvel, because it seems to each person that his own language is being spoken. But there are skeptics who attribute the uproar to drunkenness. Practical Peter explains. First, he points out that it is nine in the morning—too early to be drunk! Next, with frequent references to the Old Testament, he proclaims Jesus as the fulfillment of all earlier hopes of salvation, and calls upon his listeners to repent and be saved. His homespun eloquence proves very moving. About three thousand are baptized that day.

There follows an idyllic but brief period when everything is going well. The believers constantly meet for prayer and the breaking of bread; their economy is a primitive communism, with each giving his possessions into a common store. The general public, for the moment, approves of them, and new converts stream in every day.

The golden times do not last. In chapter 4 Peter and John are questioned by the high priest, who receives a short sermon on the meaning of Christ as his reward. The priestly party knows it must move cautiously, for all Jerusalem is buzzing with news of a miraculous healing by Peter. Somewhat lamely the persecutors command the disciples not to speak or teach in the name of Jesus, but Peter and John reply (Acts 4:19-20*): " 'Is it right in God's eyes for us to obey you rather than God? Judge for yourselves. We cannot possibly give up speaking of things we have seen and heard.' " Fearing the reactions of the crowds, the persecutors merely repeat their warning and release the prisoners.

In chapter 5, the apostles are again arrested and are brought before the full Sanhedrin. It is an impasse. The High Priest reminds them that they have been ordered to keep silent about Jesus. Peter replies that they must obey God, not man. A Pharisee named Gamaliel urges caution; it is just possible that these strange men are speaking for God. For once, their enemies seem to feel a trace of uncertainty. They content themselves with flogging the prisoners and once more commanding silence. The apostles leave, rejoicing that they have been privileged to suffer the indignity of a whipping out of loyalty to Jesus.

Soon after this we have the story of the first martyr, the deacon Stephen. He is brought before the Sanhedrin on charges of blasphemy against God and Moses. When asked to defend himself, he gives a long sermon, tracing sacred history from Abraham to the coming of Jesus, and concluding (Acts 7:51-60):

> "How stubborn you are, heathen still at heart and deaf to the truth! You always fight against the Holy Spirit. Like fathers, like sons. Was there ever a prophet whom your fathers did not persecute? They killed those who foretold the coming of the Righteous One; and now you have betrayed him and murdered him, you who received the Law as God's angels gave it to you, and yet have not kept it."

This touched them on the raw and they ground their teeth with fury. But Stephen, filled with the Holy Spirit, and gazing intently

---

* Biblical quotations in this chapter are from the New English Bible.

up to heaven, saw the glory of God, and Jesus standing at God's right hand. "Look," he said, "there is a rift in the sky; I can see the Son of Man standing at God's right hand!" At this they gave a great shout and stopped their ears. Then they made one rush at him and, flinging him out of the city, set about stoning him. The witnesses laid their coats at the feet of a young man named Saul. So they stoned Stephen, and as they did so, he called out, "Lord Jesus, receive my spirit." Then he fell on his knees and cried aloud, "Lord, do not hold this sin against them," and with that he died. And Saul was among those who approved of his murder.

This act of lynch law—no one could be legally put to death without the consent of the Roman authorities—touches off a period of violent persecution. Many Christians flee from Jerusalem. Saul is one of the main persecutors. However, he is approaching a turning point. It is vividly described in Acts 9:1-9:

> Meanwhile Saul was still breathing murderous threats against the disciples of the Lord. He went to the High Priest and applied for letters to the synagogues at Damascus authorizing him to arrest anyone he found, men or women, who followed the new way, and bring them to Jerusalem. While he was still on the road and nearing Damascus, suddenly a light flashed from the sky all around him. He fell to the ground and heard a voice saying, "Saul, Saul, why do you persecute me?" "Tell me, Lord," he said, "who you are." The voice answered, "I am Jesus, whom you are persecuting. But get up and go into the city, and you will be told what you have to do." Meanwhile the men who were travelling with him stood speechless; they heard the voice but could see no one. Saul got up from the ground, but when he opened his eyes he could not see; so they led him by the hand and brought him into Damascus. He was blind for three days, and took no food or drink.

From now on, he will promote the Nazarene faith with the same unflagging zeal he earlier displayed in persecuting the Christians.

At this early period, there is the unresolved question of what to do with gentile converts (chapter 10). Did they first have to become Jews? Did they need to be circumcised and obey the full Law, including its dietary requirements? Peter has a vision that answers these questions. He sees a great sheet in the sky and watches it as it is lowered to the ground. Inside are edible creatures of every kind. A voice commands: "Up, Peter, kill and eat." Aghast, Peter cries out that he has never eaten anything unclean or profane. The voice speaks again, telling him not to call anything unclean if God considers it clean. Soon a messenger arrives from a religious gentile who wants Peter to come to his home and bring the message of Jesus. Peter now readily consents, for his vision has convinced him that the doors must be flung wide open for all peoples. He summarizes the Christian message, and suddenly the Holy Spirit comes upon them all and they begin to speak in tongues. Peter promptly baptizes the household.

When Peter returns to Jerusalem (chapter 11) some of the disciples are disturbed. After all, Peter has been visiting uncircumcised men. He defends himslef by recounting his vision. The critics are momentarily won over. They praise God who has granted repentance even to the gentiles.

The dilemma of whether to accept converts without requiring circumcision comes up again (chapter 15). A conference is convened in Jerusalem to settle the matter. Peter speaks eloquently, pointing out that the Hebrews have never been able to obey the Law completely, and it is an impossible burden for gentile converts. In any case, he makes clear, salvation is not from obedience to the Law, but comes by the grace of Jesus. James finally proposes a statement advising gentile converts to refrain from anything polluted by contact with idols and from strangled food, blood, and fornication, but makes no demand that they be circumcised or observe the Law in all its complexity. At this moment, perhaps, the young church took the crucial step which with time would make it impossible for the Nazarene movement to function simply as one "school of thought" among many in the framework of the Jewish religion. To treat the Law as optional was to strike, however unintentionally, at the very heart of the Jewish faith. Christianity would always retain profound traces of its Jewish origin, cherishing the same Old Testament, but the two faiths would go their separate ways.

There is not time to deal with all Paul's voyages and the adventures along the way. But I cannot forego singling out his stay in Athens (chapter 17). The scene is incomparably convincing. We see the ancient city, now no great military power but still carrying on its tradition of intellectual inquiry. Citizens and visitors alike do little except discuss philosophy. To them, Paul is just one more philosopher with a strange god called Resurrection. He is invited to come to Mars Hill and give an exposition of his philosophy. Much as he detests idols, he uses their omnipresence as a springboard for his lecture before the Court of Areopagus (Acts 17:22–23): " 'Men of Athens, I see that in everything that concerns religion you are uncommonly scrupulous. For as I was going round looking at the objects of your worship, I noticed among other things an altar bearing the inscription "To an Unknown God." What you worship but do not know—this is what I now proclaim.' "

Paul seems to have had a mixed reception. Some scoffed; others said they would like to hear more sometime later; a few were converted.

One of Paul's most successful missions was in the city of Ephesus, where he soon had converts streaming in. But wherever he went, trouble erupted. This time he was threatening the economic wellbeing of the city, which depended on the manufacture of small silver shrines of the goddess Diana and the influx of tourists to see the great temple. A prosperous silversmith arouses the population to a fury of self-interest. A mob roars its way into the theater, shouting "Great is Diana of the Ephesians." After two hours of this, the town clerk finally calms them down and a riot is averted.

Not long afterward we find Paul back in Jerusalem. His presence arouses mob fury. The armed forces move in to control the situation, and Paul is taken into protective custody. He asks, and receives, permission to speak. He describes his early career as a merciless foe of the Nazarenes. Then he comes to his experience on the road to Damascus. The crowd grows threatening. The commandant orders him brought into the barracks and is about to flog him to make him explain his actions. Paul breaks the news that he is a Roman citizen and not subject to this treatment. Next day he is taken before the Sanhedrin.

Quickly recognizing that they are a mixed group of Pharisees and Sadducees, he cleverly gets the two factions into an argument over the resurrection of the dead. In the heat of the debate, some Pharisees actually come to Paul's defense.

Next he is taken before the Governor, Felix, and seizes the opportunity to exonerate himself. Again he maintains that the real controversy is over the resurrection of the dead. Later the Governor seeks Paul out to hear him talk about Jesus, but abruptly suspends the conversation when Paul begins to speak of morality, self-control, and the final judgment.

After appearing before a succession of courts, Paul exercises his right as a Roman citizen, and appeals his case to Caesar. Then begins his perilous voyage to Italy, which was discussed in an earlier chapter. When the ship finally reaches Italy and Paul travels to Rome, he is met by delegations of Christians who come out to welcome him.

Paul's most amazing missionary work now commences, during the two-year period he is under house arrest. He rents lodgings, shared by a soldier who keeps track of him. Not losing any time, Paul invites the local Jewish leaders to hear him to learn why he is a prisoner. They reply that they have not heard anything to his discredit, but no one has anything good to say about his sect. Paul and the leaders agree upon a day, and large numbers come. All day long he presents the Christian case. As usual, some are won over and others remain unconvinced.

Paul continues to receive all who find their way to his lodgings, giving them the familiar Christian message. He has the most peaceful two years he has known since the road to Damascus. Such is the closing scene of Acts.

What happened after the two years? Somewhere along the way he was put to death. At least, by the end of the first century, we find him listed as one of the great martyrs of the Church. Thus finally ended the life of the man who, next to Jesus himself, had the most to do with shaping the future of Christianity and spreading the Church worldwide.

※ 29 ※

An Early Christian Letter
(Act Four, continued)

Probably as soon as the four gospels were set down in writing an air of authority emanated from them. They were the nearest thing to an official account of the origin and nature of the Christian faith. But gradually, letters by early Church leaders (earlier than the gospels in their present form) began to turn up at various churches where they had been treasured. These have a variety of authors, in some cases still debated by scholars, but Paul apparently was the most prolific writer of "epistles." His letters are invaluable in two different ways. They give us our clearest picture of church life in the early days of Christianity, and they have profoundly shaped the theological understanding of the faith.

1 Corinthians will serve as a typical epistle, dealing both with practical problems of church life and questions of theology. We quickly learn that conversion does not automatically make moral paragons of the new members. In chapter 5 Paul says that one of the church members at Corinth is sleeping with his father's wife. Paul warns that such corruption can spread and destroy the integrity of the church. Unless the offender repents, he must be expelled. Paul then goes on to explain that he is not ordering the believers to apply the same standard to pagans, otherwise they would have to withdraw from the world altogether. He is concerned here only with the purity of life inside the Christian brotherhood.

In chapter 6, Paul expresses his horror when he learns that church members are taking their disagreements to the secular courts. Surely it ought to be possible to resolve these problems inside the church, without submitting to the judgment of outsiders.

In the same chapter, Paul attacks head-on the libertines who believe that since the coming of Christ, all things are permitted. He singles out fornication, which is a sin against one's own body, the Temple of the Holy Spirit. This is followed in the next chapter by answers to various questions that have been submitted to him. He talks about the obligations within marriage, and the advisability of remarriage in the case of widows. He would prefer that everyone be like him, unmarried, but he grants that this is too heavy a strain for many. His discussion of marriage was probably shaped by his conviction, which he shared with most early Christians, that Christ might return any day, and that meanwhile marriage was an extra responsibility, making it more difficult to prepare for the ultimate moment now so close at hand.

In chapter 8, Paul comes to a problem that must have been a serious dilemma to Christians living in a pagan city where sacrifices were constantly being offered to idols. Apparently this food was then consumed at feasts in the pagan temples. Paul opposes participation on psychological grounds. Of course, the pagan gods are figments of imagination, and the meat in itself is harmless—but anyone taking part in these feasts is in danger of having his faith weakened by the surroundings. Still more to the point, he sets a dangerous example for his weaker brother who may still be half-pagan at heart. Thus, for reasons of Christian solicitude, it is better not to exercise too much freedom. By refraining from the meat, one strengthens the faith of the faltering.

Next, in chapter 11, come the famous words about women in church and why they should cover their heads. It is based candidly on a hierarchal view of creation (God as head of Christ, Christ as head of man, man as head of woman) and resounds with the resonance of male chauvinism, when read from a late twentieth-century perspective. However, it is not a simple chauvinism. Paul concedes in 1 Corinthians 11:11–12*: "And yet, in Christ's fellowship woman is as essential to man as man to woman. If woman was made out of man, it is through woman that man now comes to be; and God is the source of all."

---

* Biblical quotations in this chapter are from the New English Bible.

In partial if not complete vindication of Paul, one can turn to historical sociology—in particular the fact that women with uncovered heads were likely to be prostitutes. The symbolism of a woman without hat or shawl was jarring. Probably, however, Paul does indeed see the question as theological rather than sociological. Although he views the relation of man and woman in hierarchal terms, few writers have so eloquently pictured the commitment of marriage and the mutual obligations, supremely love and solicitude, that ought to prevail.

Many Christians, reflecting on the drab tone and frequent bickering of their local church, have been tempted to romanticize the pristine days of the church when it existed, sparkling new, as a half hidden fellowship meeting in members' homes. Surely, one thinks, it must have been a more inspiring expression of Christ than the imposing but spiritually empty church down the street. At the very least, those early Christians must have broken bread and drunk sacramental wine in a spirit of holy reverence. Not so, Paul says. In chapter 11 he talks of Christians meeting for an *agape* meal followed by Holy Communion. Apparently many communicants bring along their own food and wolf it down while the poorer members look on hungry and embarrassed. He even speaks of some who get drunk. It does not sound like a very loving or reverent occasion. Paul goes on to describe how Christ instituted the sacrament on the very night that he was handed over to his enemies. Anyone who receives Holy Communion lightly is demeaning the very body of Christ. Each participant should carefully search his thoughts and soul before consuming the sacred bread and wine. And that is precisely what some, at least, of the church members at Corinth have not been doing.

In the next couple of chapters, Paul turns away from these disciplinary problems to launch into a long discussion of spiritual gifts. He sees the Church in organic rather than social-contract terms. All believers, taken together, are like a human body with its diversity of organs. I may be a foot, so to speak; you may be an eye. Each member brings his special gifts to the total body. There is thus a kind of divine specialization within the church: one person is called to be a healer, another to preach, and so forth. The Spirit works through all these specialists.

Still, Paul says there is one gift of the Spirit that all should strive for, no matter what one's specialized talent may be. That is the gift of love. Paul here uses the Greek word, *agape*, originally a general word for love which in the mouths of the early Christians came to mean the kind of outgoing and undemanding love and concern for others that God has for his creation. If one thinks of Paul as a grim person, it comes as a surprise to encounter the beauty and eloquence of his hymn to love as the supreme virtue and gift (1 Corinthians 13:1–13):

> I may speak in tongues of men or of angels, but if I am without love, I am a sounding gong or a clanging cymbal. I may have the gift of prophecy, and know every hidden truth; I may have faith strong enough to move mountains; but if I have no love, I am nothing. I may dole out all I possess, or even give my body to be burnt, but if I have no love, I am none the better.
>
> Love is patient; love is kind and envies no one. Love is never boastful, nor conceited, nor rude; never selfish, not quick to take offence. Love keeps no score of wrongs; does not gloat over other men's sins, but delights in the truth. There is nothing love cannot face; there is no limit to its faith, its hope, and its endurance.
>
> Love will never come to an end. Are there prophets? their work will be over. Are there tongues of ecstasy? they will cease. Is there knowledge? it will vanish away; for our knowledge and our prophecy alike are partial, and the partial vanishes when wholeness comes. When I was a child, my speech, my outlook, and my thoughts were all childish. When I grew up, I had finished with childish things. Now we see only puzzling reflections in a mirror, but then we shall see face to face. My knowledge now is partial; then it will be whole, like God's knowledge of me. In a word, there are three things that last for ever: faith, hope, and love; but the greatest of them all is love.

Paul aims at encouraging a balance in church life (chapter 14). Love is the highest attainment, but other gifts are important too, such as the gift to prophecy. It can edify and instruct the church. More of a problem is the question of speaking in tongues. Paul does not try to exclude it, but wants to ensure that it does not run wild and turn the church into what will seem, to outsiders, a congregation of madmen. He lays down guidelines and emphasizes that preaching in a language everybody understands is more useful than speaking in unknown tongues.

In chapter 15 Paul speaks of the resurrection of the dead and reaches heights of eloquence matched only by his poem on the primacy of love. Apparently some of the Corinthian Christians have lost faith—if they ever had it—in the resurrection of Christ and the general resurrection. He insists in 1 Corinthians 15:12-19:

> Now if this is what we proclaim, that Christ was raised from the dead, how can some of you say there is no resurrection of the dead? If there be no resurrection, then Christ was not raised; and if Christ was not raised, then our gospel is null and void, and so is your faith; and we turn out to be lying witnesses for God, because we bore witness that he raised Christ to life, whereas, if the dead are not raised, he did not raise him. For if the dead are not raised, it follows that Christ was not raised; and if Christ was not raised, your faith has nothing in it and you are still in your old state of sin. It follows also that those who have died within Christ's fellowship are utterly lost. If it is for this life only that Christ has given us hope, we of all men are most to be pitied.

After this powerful theological statement, Paul proceeds to deal with some of the questions the Corinthians have been asking. They want to know *how* the dead are raised, and what sort of bodies they have. These are stupid questions, Paul says bluntly. He explains that the resurrection body is not a replica of the earthly body. It is a glorified and transfigured body. Paul's own words say it best (1 Corinthians 15:39-44):

> All flesh is not the same flesh: there is flesh of men, flesh of beasts, of birds, and of fishes—all different. There are heavenly bodies and earthly bodies; and the splendour of the heavenly bodies is one thing, the splendour of the earthly, another. The sun has a splendour of its own, the moon another splendour, and the stars another, for star differs from star in brightness. So it is with the resurrection of the dead. What is sown in the earth as a perishable thing is raised imperishable. Sown in humiliation, it is raised in glory; sown in weakness, it is raised in power; sown as an animal body, it is raised as a spiritual body.

A few paragraphs farther on, Paul soars into a hymn of Thanksgiving (1 Corinthians 15:54-58):

And when our mortality has been clothed with immortality, then the saying of Scripture will come true: "Death is swallowed up; victory is won!" "O Death, where is your victory? O Death, where is your sting?" The sting of death is sin, and sin gains its power from the law; but, God be praised, he gives us the victory through our Lord Jesus Christ.

The whole epistle has a rising rhythm to it. It begins with practical advice about the Christian life and the role of the church, and disposes in short order of many controversies. But Paul's greatest eloquence is aroused not by these fussy and inevitable problems, but by such majestic themes as the supremacy of love and the fact and meaning of resurrection. Here he takes wings and flies into the upper reaches of the spirit. Far below, the church at Corinth is no doubt continuing its accustomed life, perhaps a little chastened and even a trifle reformed from Paul's sternly loving admonitions. But the ultimate hope he holds out to them is not simply a moral and decent life—though he assumes that—but a life as transformed as a worm changed into a butterfly. In that realm of existence Paul is firmly anchored, and he waits with absolute confidence for the day when Christ will remake the world and commit it into the hands of the Father.

❧ 30 ❧

To the Romans
(Act Four, concluded)

We saw earlier that formal theology is rare in the Old Testament. The emphasis on events rather than doctrines is still characteristic of the Jewish approach to religion. I remember asking one rabbi something about "Jewish theology," and he confessed that the phrase made him uneasy; he would be more at home with "Jewish sociology."

The first three gospels are more explicitly theological than most of the Old Testament; even so, what remains most vividly in the reader's mind is a series of compelling events. John is the most theological of the gospels, but its author still does not attempt a systematic statement and analysis of Christian belief. Mainly, he drives home a few profound ideas, centering around Jesus as Son of God and Word of God—the one whose death and resurrection have brought into existence a new relation with God.

Meanwhile, before the gospels (as we now know them) were circulated, Paul was busy becoming the first systematic theologian of the young Church. His background and temperament hardly left him a choice. A man with a passion to find truth and understand it, he had an excellent rabbinical training and was steeped in the Hebrew scriptures. Since he grew up in a Greek-speaking city, he also had some familiarity with Greek philosophy. If anyone was equipped to probe the sometimes vague intuitions that the early Christians had about the titanic events they had witnessed, it was Paul. And he was a man with a compulsion to share whatever comprehension he had. He could spend much time on practical problems, as in 1 Corinthians, but his greatest literary zeal was inspired when he endeavored to provide a step-by-step understanding of the Christian faith and how it related to the revelation of the Old Testament.

In the Epistle to the Romans, Paul is writing to a church he has never visited, and thus is freed from the multitude of little questions and problems that so often consumed his time. Romans needs to be supplemented by Paul's other letters in order to piece together his theology, but by itself it at least indicates how he understood the sweep of divine history from the time of Adam to the time of Jesus.

When Paul wrote Romans, he was hoping to visit the imperial city on his way to Spain where he intended to carry on missionary work. There was already a flourishing Roman church, partly Jewish and partly gentile in origin, and he wished to become acquainted with it. The epistle was advance preparation for a visit, to acquaint the Roman Christians with his understanding of the faith. Eventually, he did indeed arrive in Rome, but as a prisoner in chains.

It is impossible to overstate the impact of this epistle. It is an enduring foundation of Christian theological thinking. Time after time it has played a crucial role in inspiring new understandings of Christianity. Augustine, Luther, Karl Barth—these are only three who have felt its probing impact. Books the length of an unabridged dictionary have been written about Romans. All one can attempt here is a brief survey of its high points, in the hope of grasping its main themes.*

After the initial greetings in chapter 1, Paul briefly states his theme (Romans 1:16–17**):

> For I am not ashamed of the Gospel. It is the saving power of God for everyone who has faith—the Jew first, but the Greek also—because here is revealed God's way of righting wrong, a way that starts from faith and ends in faith; as Scripture says, "he shall gain life who is justified through faith."

The central theme has now been stated. Faith. Having established it, Paul goes on to paint an appalling picture of ordinary

---

*A biblical commentary, such as William Neil, *Harper's Bible Commentary* (New York: Harper & Row, 1962), is helpful at this point. I have incorporated some insights from this book.

**Biblical quotations in this chapter are from the New English Bible.

pagan life. Its corruption comes about because the pagans refuse to recognize the true God, though his reality, manifested through his creation, is clear enough. Since their relation with God is wrong or nonexistent, they have no center to their lives, and drift along in moral blindness (Romans 1:18–32).

So much for the Greeks. But the Jews are not any better off. For the next couple of chapters Paul cautions them against presuming on their special relation with God. Don't pass judgment on the gentiles, he says. You live no better than they, and so you will really be judging yourself. Knowing the Law is not the important thing; *keeping* it is what counts. Pagans who do not know the Law but listen to their conscience actually have the Law engraved on their hearts. The person who boasts of possessing the Law needs to teach himself first. Instead, he often preaches against stealing and then steals; inveighs against adultery and goes off to practice it. The long and the short of it is that Jew and gentile alike are under the power of sin, and by their own unaided efforts they cannot liberate themselves from it.

Paul, now in the middle of chapter 3, talks of God's justice. In some versions of the Bible the word righteousness is used. In any case, it means God's redemptive activities. The same righteousness that was earlier revealed through the Law is now made evident to everyone who has faith in Jesus Christ. Christ gave his life to reconcile God and man. Thus a person is placed in the right relation with God (justified) if he comes to Christ in faith. By God's grace, he is accepted.

Paul is now ready to state the role of faith in one brief passage (Romans 3:27–31):

> What room then is left for human pride? It is excluded. And on what principle? The keeping of the law would not exclude it, but faith does. For our argument is that a man is justified by faith quite apart from success in keeping the law.
>
> Do you suppose God is the God of the Jews alone? Is he not the God of Gentiles also? Certainly, of Gentiles also, if it be true that God is one. And he will therefore justify both the circumcised in virtue of their faith, and the uncircumcised through their faith. Does this mean that we are using faith to undermine law? By no means: we are placing law itself on a firmer footing.

Next, he chooses the traditional ancestor of the Hebrews, Abraham, to drive home the primacy of faith. In chapter 4 he points out that Abraham was justified in the sight of God not because of a good life, but because of his trust in God. This was at a time when he had not yet been circumcised (and, of course, the Mosaic Law lay centuries in the future). No law put him in right relation with God. Faith did.

Another strand that runs through Paul's thought is the concept of Jesus as the new Adam, coming to earth to undo the harm accomplished by the symbolic ancestor of all humankind. In chapter 5 he describes how sin and death came through Adam, but Christ has more than made up for the harm thus done. Once there was sin and death; now there is grace and life.

One of the perils of liberation from the Law is that people could easily leap to the conclusion that "Anything goes." Paul emphasizes in chapter 6 that this is a crude misunderstanding. We are not called upon to sin so that God's grace will have wider scope. In baptism we share Christ's death and rise to a new life. The slate is wiped clean and we are free to be the slaves of God and participate in Christ's eternal life.

One striking paragraph shows deep psychological penetration, as Paul depicts the struggle waged within (Romans 7:14–25):

> We know that the law is spiritual; but I am not: I am unspiritual, the purchased slave of sin. I do not even acknowledge my own actions as mine, for what I do is not what I want to do, but what I detest. But if what I do is against my will, it means that I agree with the law and hold it to be admirable. But as things are, it is no longer I who perform the action, but sin that lodges in me. For I know that nothing good lodges in me—in my unspiritual nature, I mean—for though the will to do good is there, the deed is not. The good which I want to do, I fail to do; but what I do is the wrong which is against my will; and if what I do is against my will, clearly it is no longer I who am the agent, but sin that has its lodging in me.
>
> I discover this principle, then: that when I want to do the right, only the wrong is within my reach. In my inmost self I delight in the law of God, but I perceive that there is in my bodily members a

different law, fighting against the law that my reason approves and making me a prisoner under the law that is in my members, the law of sin. Miserable creature that I am, who is there to rescue me out of this body doomed to death? God alone, through Jesus Christ our Lord! Thanks be to God! In a word then, I myself, subject to God's law as a rational being, am yet, in my unspiritual nature, a slave to the law of sin.

In chapter 8, Paul comes to another of his peaks of eloquence when he triumphantly proclaims (Romans 8:31–39):

> With all this in mind, what are we to say? If God is on our side, who is against us? He did not spare his own Son, but gave him up for us all; and with this gift how can he fail to lavish upon us all he has to give? Who will be the accuser of God's chosen ones? It is God who pronounces acquittal; then who can condemn? It is Christ— Christ who died, and, more than that, was raised from the dead— who is at God's right hand, and indeed pleads our cause. Then what can separate us from the love of Christ? Can affliction or hardship? Can persecution, hunger, nakedness, peril, or the sword? "We are being done to death for thy sake all day long," as Scripture says; "we have been treated like sheep for slaughter"—and yet, in spite of all, overwhelming victory is ours through him who loved us. For I am convinced that there is nothing in death or life, in the realm of spirits or superhuman powers, in the world as it is or the world as it shall be, in the forces of the universe, in heights or depths—nothing in all creation that can separate us from the love of God in Christ Jesus our Lord.

Up to this point, Paul has been dealing off and on with the special mission of the Jews. Now, in chapter 9, he focuses on that question. He begins with a passionate statement of his love for the Chosen People. He even says he would be willing to be cut off from Christ if that would help his brothers of Israel. He lists the elements of their uniqueness: the special relation with God, the covenants, the Law, most of all, the people from whom Christ was descended.

Paul emphatically rejects any idea that the Jews have been renounced by God. His Old Testament promises are still binding, but if they are properly understood they point toward Christ, who came not for the sake of gentiles only, nor for Jews only, but for all. The same message is addressed to Jews as to gentiles—have faith and you will be put in right relation to God, thanks to his grace. Paul thus sees conversion to Christianity as the ultimate fulfillment of age-old hopes and longings. Meanwhile, the Jews remain a Chosen People, and gentile Christians draw life from the deep Jewish roots of their faith.

With the end of chapter 11, the main part of this epistle concludes. One can imagine Paul with an outline in front of him, checking off one item after another. But he still has some things to say that do not fit into a formal theological treatise. He continues writing or dictating in the fluent Greek he had learned as a boy. Paul brings up one of his most typical themes: the diversity of gifts. Cultivate the one you have, he says, and don't look down on people with different gifts. Love one another; if trials come, don't give up; bless your enemies, make friends with the poor; obey the civil authorities, for their function is from God.

Then in one paragraph he answers those who have wondered what guidance they have in their daily lives now that the Law is dethroned (Romans 13:8b–10):

> He who loves his neighbor has satisfied every claim of the law. For the commandments, "Thou shalt not commit adultery, thou shalt not kill, thou shalt not steal, thou shalt not covet," and any other commandments there may be, are all summed up in the one rule, "Love your neighbor as yourself." Love cannot wrong a neighbor; therefore the whole law is summed up in love.

In other words, the moral life is a love story. All else is commentary.

If somewhere along the way in Romans the reader finds himself confused, there is ample enough reason. Paul's mind was an intricate one, and his way of approaching theological questions is often different from ours. Still, it ought to be possible to summarize briefly the main message he tries to convey in the epistle.

Man's fundamental problem, as Paul sees it, is his alienation from God. The Hebrew Law has not been able to cure this. Rather, its main value is to show us, through our failures to live up to it, how deep the alienation is. Neither Judaism nor paganism has the key to a new and redeemed life. Who can stand in the presence of the infinitely holy God? If we cannot ascend to God, he must descend to us. This he does in person of his son, Jesus Christ.

In the life, death and resurrection of Christ one sees the righteousness of God at work. He accepts the act of self-giving by which Christ bridges the gulf. Though we are sinners, when we turn to Christ in faith God treats us *as though* we were innocent. Therefore the Christian is not one who strains every muscle to live up to an impossibly high standard. Rather, he is one giving praises for a reconciliation with God that he could never merit or achieve on his own. His life is one long thanksgiving, and his moral code is simply the imperative of love and all that follows from love. Such a person is "justified by faith."

≫ 31 ≪

Dazzling Visions
(Act Five)

With the last chapter we come to the end of Act Four. And yet, that way of putting it misleads. The drama is not over. It continues to this very moment, for *we* are living in Act Four. As we read the Book of Acts or the epistles, we quickly discover ourselves among the ancient actors. Now as then, great empires roar and threaten. Not too much has changed. It is true that two thousand years is a long time compared to man's proverbial three score and ten, but we are told that to God it is the blinking of an eye. So, if we are Christians at all, we are early Christians.

One often thinks: How long it is taking! If God through

Christ intends the radical reshaping and transformation of the world, why is he waiting so long? Even in those periods when they were not persecuted, the first Christians anticipated the return of Christ on clouds of glory. It could happen any day. In times of cruel persecution, the hope of a direct intervention was the source of whatever confidence they could retain in God's hidden rule over even the most detestable kingdoms of this earth. But as the persecution increased, the agonized clamor for God's visible takeover grew stronger.

In the first few decades after the life of Jesus, the Romans were usually indifferent to this new Nazarene cult, until conflicts between it and its opponents threatened civil stability. Gradually the Romans launched successive campaigns of persecution on an extensive scale. To mad Nero the pyromaniac belongs the credit for the first persecution, though his motives were probably not religious; he hoped to cover up his arsonist tracks after burning down a large part of Rome. Not many years later Vespasian decreed the death penalty to all who refused to worship the image of the emperor. Toward the end of the first century, Domitian, another lunatic emperor, carried on a genocidal persecution of all Christians who refused to render homage to his divinity. It was probably during his reign, when a holocaust threatened the embattled Christians, that the Revelation of John was written.

Why should Roman emperors worry about this obscure sect? The answer is probably as much political as religious. In most situations, the Romans practiced religious tolerance. Not believing too earnestly in any god themselves, it didn't bother them to see their neighbors worshiping a variety of deities. But they did take seriously the need to safeguard and foster the internal cohesion of the vast empire. Though most Romans probably took the doctrine of the emperor's divinity with more than a grain of salt, the divine honors paid to him were a harmless way of encouraging a spirit of imperial unity. And why should these Christians object? Everyone else—except the Jews, it is true—was willing to offer a pinch of incense. This kind of mild worship of the emperor must have seemed as innocuous as saluting the flag.

However, it was not a Caesar's job to engage in theological debates with minority groups. The Roman empire at its peak—one of the most efficient ever created—was uncompromising in its use of power. It did not hesitate to bring out the scourge and the cross, or to summon wild animals. It was determined to get results, and for several centuries it was a marvel; brutal but effective.

In short, Rome was like many empires before and since. It fostered material progress and at its best maintained a surprising degree of social order. But as its might increased, its soul diminished. Perhaps in the late first century most ordinary people would have agreed that it wasn't too bad a system. At least it kept bandits under control and provided reliable transport for grain. But the Christians saw it quite differently. To them Rome was another name for monstrous, pagan Babylon.

We know almost nothing about the John who wrote Revelation. He was exiled to the penal colony of Patmos, an Aegean island, but before that one can only speculate. Almost certainly he was not the John who wrote the gospel of that name. The Greek of Revelation is ungrammatical and unidiomatic, as though the author had learned it late in life.

His literary genre was the apocalypse, common enough in both Jewish and Christian literature from about 200 B.C. to A.D. 100. In the Old Testament, Daniel is an example. Revelation is the one apocalypse accepted into the New Testament. What they all have in common is the conviction that—though God seems unable to reshape the human condition here and now—he reigns in an eternal world from which he will suddenly emerge and put an end to all suffering and sin. At that time the righteous will have their vindication. It is the kind of world-view that oppressed minorities often have. One thinks of the cargo cults of the Pacific, and even of science fiction stories in which beings from outer space play a messianic role when they suddenly appear.

It is unfortunate but probably inevitable that Revelation has fascinated many religious cranks who examine its symbolism as eagerly as their colleagues measure the pyramids, seeking hidden clues to what is going to happen in the future. John was not foreseeing the communist revolution in Russia nor the rise of China to great power status. He was concerned with matters closer to home: one specific empire (the Roman) and a particular moment in time—a major persecution of the young churches. Any prophecies he makes are within that framework. What he predicts is clear enough, however complex its symbolism. He is saying that God will destroy the mighty Roman empire and create a new world order in which the Christians who have remained steadfast will have their reward. Meanwhile, he calls upon them to increase their faith and to wait and trust. The final battle between good and evil has already been won in heaven. It will yet be won on earth also, when God like a commanding general invades this planet.

But first, each church must look at itself and see how well it is enduring the dangerous death agonies of brutal Rome. John begins with letters addressed to seven churches in the Ephesus area. They are a mixed bag. He praises the Philadelphian church for its steadfastness, while scolding Laodicea for being lukewarm. Ephesus is courageous but lacking in enthusiasm; Pergamum too much inclined to compromise. His overall message is: stand fast. Though it seems that the devil is rampant, God will have the last word and will intervene when least expected.

Abruptly, John leaves the earth and recounts a vision in which he beholds God seated in his heavenly majesty (Revelation 4:10-11*):

... The twenty-four elders prostrated themselves before him to worship the One who lives for ever and ever, and threw down their crowns in front of the throne, saying, "You are our Lord and our God, you are worthy of glory and honour and power, because you made all the universe and it was only by your will that everything was made and exists."

In the hands of God is a scroll with seven seals. A lamb, symbolizing Christ, opens it seal by seal. War, revolution, famine, and pestilence sweep over the earth—the result of mankind's

---

* Biblical quotations in this chapter are from the Jerusalem Bible.

refusal to live by God's commands. In the midst of describing these terrors, John pauses to picture the final blessedness of those who are faithful to Christ despite all torments (Revelation 7:9–17):

> After that I saw a huge number, impossible to count, of people from every nation, race, tribe and language; they were standing in front of the throne and in front of the Lamb, dressed in white robes and holding palms in their hands. They shouted aloud, "Victory to our God, who sits on the throne, and to the Lamb!" And all the angels who were standing in a circle round the throne, surrounding the elders and the four animals, prostrated themselves before the throne, and touched the ground with their foreheads, worshipping God with these words, "Amen. Praise and glory and wisdom and thanksgiving and honour and power and strength to our God for ever and ever. Amen."
>
> One of the elders then spoke, and asked me, "Do you know who these people are, dressed in white robes, and where they have come from?" I answered him, "You can tell me, my lord." Then he said, "These are the people who have been through the great persecution, and because they have washed their robes white again in the blood of the Lamb, they now stand in front of God's throne and serve him day and night in his sanctuary; and the One who sits on the throne will spread his tent over them. They will never hunger or thirst again; neither the sun nor scorching wind will ever plague them, because the Lamb who is at the throne will be their shepherd and will lead them to springs of living water; and God will wipe away all tears from their eyes."

John gradually creates a picture of the final conflict between good and evil. Though the Devil strives to alienate people from their God, the divine purposes cannot ultimately be defeated. The conflict has actually already been won by the forces of good. When Christ ascended to heaven, Satan fell. What remains on earth is God's mopping-up operation to exterminate the dominion of Satan (chapters 11 and 12). Satan's principal ally is the loathsome Roman empire.

In chapters 15 and 16 we are prepared for the ultimate battle at Armageddon. Before it occurs, imperial Rome falls, and heaven itself celebrates the destruction of the brutal persecutor. Victory is achieved, and the Devil is imprisoned (chapters 19 and 20). The messianic millennium is ushered in, followed by the final overthrow of Satan and the Last Judgment, when the dead arise to give an account of their lives.

Postscript

I come to the end of this book feeling guilty at all I have not done. Many books of the Bible were not so much as mentioned, and those that were discussed often received cursory treatment. My hope is that readers will now turn to their Bible and read it "cover to cover," with the aid of a good commentary.

I trust that this book has accomplished at least three goals. It first took random sections of the Bible and examined them as poetry, as prose narrative, as various other kinds of literature. This approach could be applied to the whole Bible, and would be fruitful throughout. The Bible *is* literature and much of it is great literature, as well as being a main source of our knowledge of ancient history and the ways of life that prevailed in those times.

Anyone completely indifferent to religion will still find the Bible a rich feast. But in our explorations of the random samples we found that an exclusively humanistic approach took us so far and no farther. The Bible began to talk back. The X-Dimension infiltrated from every side. The Bible, we discovered, is indeed literature, but a very special kind of literature. It is the revelation of how two great civilizations, the Judaic and the Christian, perceived their relation with the X-Dimension, which is another name for God.

Finally, we constructed a "mini-Bible" to help us recognize the main themes of the Bible. The theme of themes turned out to be the conviction that divine history is like a drama in which God plays the central role. Or to put it another way, that central theme is the interaction of God and man, as the scroll of time and history slowly unrolls.

As we come to see the inner meaning of history, the Bible summons us to take our places on the divine stage and act out our roles alongside the characters of the Old and New Testaments. We are their contemporaries. We converse with Adam and Eve, and we recognize with incredulous joy a rabbi who has risen from the dead. True, the Bible is great literature, and a marvelous record of ancient times and ancient ways of life. But most of all it is the record of God's deeds and the part he has reserved for us in the great drama of creation and salvation.

John now attempts to suggest a culmination that is almost beyond the power of language to express. Sin, death, and suffering are no more. The redeemed live in perfect harmony with their creator. A new Jerusalem descends from heaven to replace the old, imperfect one. This is, in fact, Eden restored. Man's long journey in exile is now ended by his return, not as a childlike creature, but as one whose redemption has been bought by God himself. All this is best said in John's words (Revelation 21:9–14):

> One of the seven angels that had the seven bowls full of the seven last plagues came to speak to me, and said, "Come here and I will show you the bride that the Lamb has married." In the spirit, he took me to the top of an enormous high mountain, and showed me Jerusalem, the holy city, coming down from God out of heaven. It had all the radiant glory of God and glittered like some precious jewel of crystal-clear diamond. The walls of it were of a great height, and had twelve gates; at each of the twelve gates there was an angel, and over the gates were written the names of the twelve tribes of Israel; on the east there were three gates, on the north three gates, on the south three gates, and on the west three gates. The city walls stood on twelve foundation stones, each one of which bore the name of one of the twelve apostles of the Lamb.

As he wrote these words, John was not thinking of men and women almost two thousand years in the future. He was picturing in symbolic terms a fulfillment beyond time and space that he expected to see inaugurated at any moment. In these hopes he was mistaken. The Roman empire had centuries of life still ahead of it. But a clear message comes from Revelation: Hold fast. The final power is not exercised by armies or committees. God has his plans for renewing the earth. It may not be by radical intervention into the daily course of life; it may come as quiet evolution. But what John tells us is that the irreversible victory over all forces of evil and alienation has already been achieved, in the realm of eternity if not yet visibly in the realm of calendars and clocks. We, living in Act Four, await Act Five. Meanwhile, we can draw strength from peering in bewildered fascination at John's vision of a redeemed humanity and a redeemed universe. As the Bible throughout affirms, God will have the last word.